FORERUNNERS: IDEAS FIRST
FROM THE UNIVERSITY OF MINNESOTA PRESS

Original e-works to spark new scholarship

Forerunners is a thought-in-process series of breakthrough digital works. Written between fresh ideas and finished books, Forerunners draws on scholarly work initiated in notable blogs, social media, conference plenaries, journal articles, and the synergy of academic exchange. This is gray literature publishing: where intense thinking, change, and speculation take place in scholarship.

John Hartigan
Aesop's Anthropology: A Multispecies Approach

Reinhold Martin
Mediators: Aesthetics, Politics, and the City

Jussi Parikka
The Anthrobscene

Steven Shaviro
No Speed Limit: Thr

NO SPEED LIMIT

No Speed Limit
Three Essays on Accelerationism

STEVEN SHAVIRO

University of Minnesota Press
Minneapolis

Published by the University of Minnesota Press, 2015
111 Third Avenue South, Suite 290
Minneapolis, MN 55401-2520
http://www.upress.umn.edu

The University of Minnesota is an equal-opportunity educator and employer.

Contents

Preface

Finally the messages penetrate
There is a corpse of an image—they penetrate
The corpse of a radio. Cocteau used a car radio on account
  of NO SPEED LIMIT. In any case the messages penetrate
  the radio and render it (and the radio) ultimately useless.

—JACK SPICER

THIS SHORT BOOK contains three essays on *accelerationism*, a concept that has been much in vogue recently. The term was first coined disparagingly in 2010 by Benjamin Noys. It has been repurposed as a positive term, most notably by Alex Williams and Nick Srnicek, in 2013, in their *Manifesto for an Accelerationist Politics*. Noys summarizes his objections to accelerationism in a recent book. Williams and Srnicek have a book forthcoming that expands upon their manifesto. The present volume occupies a kind of middle ground, in between Williams and Srnicek's advocacy and Noys's denunciation. I wish especially to consider the *aesthetic* possibilities of accelerationism.

Introduction
to Accelerationism

IN HIS SCIENCE FICTION NOVEL *Pop Apocalypse,* Lee Konstantinou imagines the existence of a "Creative Destruction" school of Marxist-Leninist thought. The adherents of this school "interpret Marx's writings as literal predictions of the future, so they consider it their mission to *help* capitalist markets spread to every corner of the world, because that's the necessary precondition for a truly socialist revolution." This means that the Creative Destruction Marxists are indistinguishable, in terms of actual practice, from the most ruthless capitalists. Their actions coincide with those of a group of investors who have concluded that "there's money to be made off the destruction of the world" and that in fact apocalyptic destruction constitutes "an unprecedented business opportunity." They therefore seek to precipitate a worldwide nuclear conflagration: "On behalf of our investors, we're obligated to take every step we can to insure that we corner the Apocalypse market before anyone else does."

Let this stand as an introductory parable of accelerationism. The term has become quite popular in the last few years, but it seems to be one of those words that has a different meaning for each person who uses it. As far as I am concerned, *accelerationism* is best defined—in political, aesthetic, and philosophical terms—as the argument that the only way out is the way through. In order to overcome globalized neoliberal capitalism, we need to drain it to the dregs, push it to its most extreme point, follow it into its furthest and strangest consequences. As Bertolt Brecht put it years ago, "Don't start from the good old things but the bad new ones." The hope is that, by exacerbating our current conditions of existence, we will finally be able to make them explode, and thereby move beyond them.

Konstantinou's description of the "Creative Destruction" Marxists is, of course, a deliberate caricature. *Pop Apocalypse* is satire, not prophecy. More generally, science fiction as a genre does not claim to actually predict the future. Rather, it works to *extrapolate* elements of the present, to consider what these elements might lead to if allowed to reach their full potential. That is to say, science fiction is not about the actual future but about the *futurity* that haunts the present. It grasps, and brings to visibility, what Deleuze calls the *virtual* dimension of existence, or what Marx calls *tendential* processes.

Science fiction takes up certain implicit conditions of our personal and social lives, and makes these conditions fully explicit in narrative. It picks out "futuristic" trends that are already embedded within our actual social and technological situation. These trends are not literal matters of fact, but they really exist *as* tendencies or potentialities. In the words of Deleuze, they are "real without being actual, ideal without being abstract, and symbolic without being fictional." They are *potentials* for change, growth, or decay, but they have not fully expressed themselves or done all that they can do. And they may not ever do so, since (as Marx points out) a tendency is always accompanied by "counteracting factors" that can inhibit or even reverse it.

In sum, the present moment contains elements of futurity, but the unfolding of these elements as actual future events is contingent and not guaranteed. A match has the potential to start a fire, but there will not be a fire if the match is never struck, or if, when struck, it is blown out by the wind. Science fiction imagines the flame, and the ensuing conflagration. It provides us with narratives in which these potentials of futurity are fully actualized, unfolding their powers to the utmost. In this way, we might say that science fiction is the accelerationist art *par excellence*, accelerationist in its very nature.

Accelerationism is a speculative movement that seeks to extrapolate the entire globalized neoliberal capitalist order. This means that it is necessarily an aesthetic movement as well as a political one. The hope driving accelerationism is that, in fully expressing the potentialities of capitalism, we will be able to exhaust it and thereby open up access to something beyond it.

Understood in this way, accelerationism has deep roots in classical Marxism. In *The Communist Manifesto*, Marx and Engels describe the production-enhancing and globalizing effects of capitalism:

In place of the old wants, satisfied by the production of the country, we find new wants, requiring for their satisfaction the products of distant lands and climes. In place of the old local and national seclusion and self-sufficiency, we have intercourse in every direction, universal inter-dependence of nations. And as in material, so also in intellectual production. The intellectual creations of individual nations become common property. National one-sidedness and narrow-mindedness become more and more impossible, and from the numerous national and local literatures, there arises a world literature. . . .

The bourgeoisie, during its rule of scarce one hundred years, has created more massive and more colossal productive forces than have all preceding generations together. Subjection of Nature's forces to man, machinery, application of chemistry to industry and agriculture, steam-navigation, railways, electric telegraphs, clearing of whole continents for cultivation, canalisation of rivers, whole populations conjured out of the ground—what earlier century had even a presentiment that such productive forces slumbered in the lap of social labour?

In all this, Marx and Engels do not sound very critical; they have even been credited with—or blamed for—sounding celebratory. However, this is not quite right. Marx's view of capitalism is dialectical, rather than moralistic. He does not oppose the creation of "new wants" or demand that we go back to the old ones. He does not condemn capitalism for being *evil*. Indeed, he hates capitalism for causing massive suffering and oppression, but he does not say that, where capitalism has mobilized new technologies, we need to reject them and return to life on a smaller scale. Rather, Marx is fascinated by the way that capitalism creates wealth and poverty simultaneously. It produces the conditions of possibility for a world of affluence and freedom *at the same time* that it produces misery and alienation. Marx is compassionate toward the victims of history and full of scathing sarcasm toward their oppressors. But he also remains relentlessly non- and antinostalgic. For him, there is no possibility of going back from capitalism's own convulsions.

Given this "parallax," or double perspective, Marx argues that capitalism tends toward a point where its very form—the property form—becomes an obstacle to the further development of the productive forces that it has unleashed:

> At a certain stage of development, the material productive forces of society come into conflict with the existing relations of production or—this merely expresses the same thing in legal terms—with the property relations within the framework of which they have operated hitherto. From forms of development of the productive forces these relations turn into their fetters. Then begins an era of social revolution.

Accelerationism finds its origin in this passage and others like it throughout Marx's writings. But of course, Marx's discussion is far from unambigious; indeed, it has been interpreted in multiple, contradictory ways. In the Hegelian language that Marx sometimes uses, capitalism negates the very being of the workers, by expropriating the fruits of their labor. But this leads to the situation in which capitalism can be overthrown by means of a "negation of the negation." That is to say, capitalism ironically creates the very conditions for, and even necessitates, its own supersession.

In the Marxist tradition, this sometimes leads to what has been disparagingly called *economism*. This is the idea that the progression from capitalism to communism is inevitable; or, in Konstantinou's words, that Marx's formulations are "literal predictions of the future." If this were the case, then all we would have to do is to wait for the dialectical contradictions of capitalism to unfold. Of course, this has never happened. If we wait for the dialectical contradictions to unfold on their own, we will find ourselves waiting forever. Despite his indebtedness to Hegel, Marx clearly does not believe that the real is rational or that the material development of society follows laws of necessity. We should rather say that, for Marx, the dictatorship of Capital is itself the realm of necessity; what's needed is somehow to get beyond it. Marx is notorious for only giving a vague sense of what life beyond the capitalist order would be like. He leaves it open as a realm for speculation, rather than giving detailed plans in the way that some of his "utopian socialist" predecessors did. By virtue of its very openness, Marx's analyses have more in common with extrapolative science fiction than they do with either Hegelian systematics or naturalistic fiction.

Given the failure of economism, many Marxists have instead gone to the opposite extreme: they have embraced a kind of voluntarism. Capitalism can be abolished by sheer force of will—as long as this is supplemented by proper methods of organization and mobilization. We see this sort of approach in the Leninist doctrine of the vanguard party, and also, I think, in the ultra-leftism of such contemporary thinkers as Slavoj Žižek and Alain Badiou. But it seems obvious to me that, over the course of the twentieth century, the voluntaristic approach fared as badly as the fatalistic one. It resulted not in human emancipation but in the horrors of Stalinism, the sclerotic tyranny of the later USSR, and the deadly convulsions of the Chinese Cultural Revolution. Today, Leninist voluntarism does not even give us that; all that remains is a fantasy of revolution, providing the basis for a self-congratulatory moralism.

The problem may be summarized as follows. Capitalism has indeed created the conditions for general prosperity and therefore for its own supersession. But it has also blocked, and continues to block, any hope of realizing this transformation. We cannot wait for capitalism to transform on its own, but we also cannot hope to progress by appealing to some radical Outside or by fashioning ourselves as militants faithful to some "event" that (as Badiou has it) would mark a radical and complete break with the given "situation" of capitalism. Accelerationism rather demands a movement against and outside capitalism—but on the basis of tendencies and technologies that are intrinsic to capitalism. Audre Lord famously argued that "the master's tools will never dismantle the master's house." But what if the master's tools are the only ones available? Accelerationism grapples with this dilemma.

What is the appeal of accelerationism today? It can be understood as a response to the particular social and political situation in which we currently seem to be trapped: that of a long-term, slow-motion catastrophe. Global warming, and environmental pollution and degradation, threaten to undermine our whole mode of life. And this mode of life is itself increasingly stressful and precarious, due to the depredations of neoliberal capitalism. As Fredric Jameson puts it, the world today is characterized by "heightened polarization, increasing unemployment, [and] the ever more desperate search for new investments and new markets." These are all general features of capitalism identified by Marx, but in neoliberal society we encounter them in a particularly pure and virulent form.

I want to be as specific as possible in my use of the term "neoliberalism" in order to describe this situation. I define neoliberalism as a specific mode of capitalist production (Marx), and form of governmentality (Foucault), that is characterized by the following specific factors:

1. The dominating influence of financial institutions, which facilitate transfers of wealth from everybody else to the already

extremely wealthy (the "One Percent" or even the top one hundredth of one percent).

2. The privatization and commodification of what used to be common or public goods (resources like water and green space, as well as public services like education, communication, sewage and garbage disposal, and transportation).

3. The extraction, by banks and other large corporations, of a surplus from all social activities: not only from production (as in the classical Marxist model of capitalism) but from circulation and consumption as well. Capital accumulation proceeds not only by direct exploitation but also by rent-seeking, by debt collection, and by outright expropriation ("primitive accumulation").

4. The subjection of all aspects of life to the so-called discipline of the market. This is equivalent, in more traditional Marxist terms, to the "real subsumption" by capital of all aspects of life: leisure as well as labor. Even our sleep is now organized in accordance with the imperatives of production and capital accumulation.

5. The redefinition of human beings as private owners of their own "human capital." Each person is thereby, as Michel Foucault puts it, forced to become "an entrepreneur of himself." In such circumstances, we are continually obliged to market ourselves, to "brand" ourselves, to maximize the return on our "investment" in ourselves. There is never enough: like the Red Queen, we always need to keep running, just to stay in the same place. *Precarity* is the fundamental condition of our lives.

All of these processes work on a global scale; they extend far beyond the level of immediate individual experience. My life is precarious, at every moment, but I cannot apprehend the forces that make it so. I know how little money is left from my last paycheck, but I cannot grasp, in concrete terms, how "the economy" works. I directly experience the daily weather, but I do not directly experience the climate. Global warming and worldwide financial networks are examples of what the ecological theorist Timothy Morton calls *hyperobjects*. They are phenomena that actually exist but that "stretch our ideas of time and space, since they far outlast most human time scales, or they're massively distributed in terrestrial space and so are unavailable to immediate experience."

Hyperobjects affect everything that we do, but we cannot point to them in specific instances. The chains of causality are far too complicated and intermeshed for us to follow. In order to make sense of our condition, we are forced to deal with difficult abstractions. We have to rely upon data that are gathered in massive quantities by scientific instruments and then collated through mathematical and statistical formulas but that are not directly accessible to our senses. We find ourselves, as Mark Hansen puts it, entangled "within networks of media technologies that operate predominantly, if not almost entirely, outside the scope of human modes of awareness (consciousness, attention, sense perception, etc.)." We cannot *imagine* such circumstances in any direct or naturalistic way, but only through the extrapolating lens of science fiction.

Subject to these conditions, we live under relentless environmental and financial assault. We continually find ourselves in what might well be called a state of crisis. However, this involves a paradox. A *crisis*—whether economic, ecological, or political—is a turning point, a sudden rupture, a sharp and immediate moment of reckoning. But for us today, crisis has become a chronic and seemingly permanent condition. We live, oxymoronically, in a state of perpetual, but never resolved, convulsion and contradiction. Crises never come to a culmination; instead, they are endlessly and indefinitely deferred.

For instance, after the economic collapse of 2008, the big banks were bailed out by the United States government. This allowed them to resume the very practices—the creation of arcane financial instruments, in order to enable relentless rent-seeking—that led to the breakdown of the economic system in the first place. The functioning of the system is restored, but only in such a way as to guarantee the renewal of the same crisis, on a greater scale, further down the road. Marx rightly noted that crises are endemic to capitalism. But far from threatening the system as Marx hoped, today these crises actually help it to renew itself. As David Harvey puts it, it is precisely "through the destruction of the achievements of preceding eras by way of war, the devaluation of assets, the degradation of productive capacity, abandonment and other forms of 'creative destruction'" that capitalism creates "a new basis for profit-making and surplus absorption."

What lurks behind this analysis is the frustrating sense of an impasse. Among its other accomplishments, neoliberal capitalism has also robbed us of the future. For it turns everything into an eternal present. The highest values of our society—as preached in the business schools—are novelty, innovation, and creativity. And yet these always only result in more of the same. How often have we been told that a minor software update "changes everything"? Our society seems to function, as Ernst Bloch once put it, in a state of "sheer aimless infinity and incessant changeability; where everything ought to be constantly new, everything remains just as it was."

This is because, in our current state of affairs, the future exists only in order to be colonized and made into an investment opportunity. John Maynard Keynes sought to distinguish between risk and genuine uncertainty. Risk is calculable in terms of probability, but genuine uncertainty is not. Uncertain events are irreducible to probabilistic analysis, because "there is no scientific basis on which to form any calculable probability whatever." Keynes's discussion of uncertainty has strong affinities with Quentin Meillassoux's account of hyperchaos. For Meillassoux, there is no "totality of cases," no closed set of all possible states of the universe. Therefore, there is no way to assign fixed probabilities to these states. This is not just an empirical matter of insufficient information; uncertainty exists *in principle*. For Meillassoux and Keynes alike, there comes a point where "we simply do not know."

But today, Keynes's distinction is entirely ignored. The Black-Scholes Formula and the Efficient Market Hypothesis both conceive the future entirely in probabilistic terms. In these theories, as in the actual financial trading that is guided by them (or at least rationalized by them), the genuine unknowability of the future is transformed into a matter of calculable, manageable risk. True novelty is excluded, because all possible outcomes have already been calculated and paid for in terms of the present. While this belief in the calculability of the future is delusional, it nonetheless determines the way that financial markets actually work.

We might therefore say that speculative finance is the inverse—and the complement—of the "affirmative speculation" that takes place in science fiction. Financial speculation seeks to capture, and shut down, the very same extreme potentialities that science fiction explores. Science fiction is the narration of open, unaccountable futures; derivatives trading claims to have *accounted for,* and *discounted,* all these futures already.

The "market"—nearly deified in neoliberal doctrine—thus works preemptively, as a global practice of what Richard

Grusin calls *premediation*. It seeks to deplete the future in advance. Its relentless functioning makes it nearly impossible for us to conceive of any alternative to the global capitalist world order. Such is the condition that Mark Fisher calls *capitalist realism*. As Fisher puts it, channeling both Jameson and Žižek, "it's easier to imagine the end of the world than the end of capitalism."

Accelerationism claims to offer a way out of this economic and imaginative impasse. It argues that we must meet the deadlock head on. We cannot escape the global "network society" by rejecting the latest technologies and retreating back to a supposedly simpler and better time. We need to embrace, and even extend, the abstractions of capitalist modernity, if we are ever to do anything about them. We cannot put a stop to environmental catastrophe and economic exploitation by adopting "small is beautiful" localism (E. F. Schumacher) or by building "a bridge to the eighteenth century" (Neil Postman). We cannot escape complexity by simplifying. We cannot secede from multinational capitalism, because it is everywhere and nowhere—just like the (heavily polluted) air that we must of necessity breathe.

The actual term *accelerationism* was first used by Benjamin Noys in his 2010 book *The Persistence of the Negative*. Noys coined the word in order to designate a certain philosophical current that has its roots in French philosophy of the 1960s and 1970s: philosophy associated especially with the events of May 1968. The failed uprising of that date was an important reference point for Gilles Deleuze and Félix Guattari, and for Jean-François Lyotard; it remains one for Badiou today.

In the early 1970s, books like Deleuze and Guattari's *Anti-Oedipus* and Lyotard's *Libidinal Economy* take up Marx and Engels's invocation of capitalism's revolutionizing power, the ways that it destroys all traditions and all certainties. Deleuze and Guattari argue that capitalism is founded upon a "twofold movement of decoding or deterritorializing flows on the one hand, and their violent and artificial reterritorialization on the other." Lyotard, less ambiguously, rhapsodizes over how the factory workers enlisted by nineteenth-century capitalism supposedly "enjoyed the decomposition of their personal identity, the identity that the peasant tradition had constructed for them, enjoyed the dissolution of their families and villages, and enjoyed the new monstrous *anonymity* of the suburbs and the pubs in the morning and evening."

It is worth noting that Deleuze and Guattari's account of capitalism's revolutionizing power—if not Lyotard's—has been widely misunderstood. Their notorious, most extreme and most quoted "accelerationist" passage urges us

> to go still further . . . in the movement of the market, of decoding and deterritorialization . . . For perhaps the flows are not yet deterritorialized enough, not decoded enough, from the viewpoint of a theory and practice of a highly schizophrenic character. Not to withdraw from the process, but to go further, to "accelerate the process," as Nietzsche put it: in this matter, the truth is that we haven't seen anything yet.

This passage has in fact been taken out of context and interpreted much more broadly than Deleuze and Guattari ever intended. It is true that, at least to a certain extent, the passage was meant as a provocation. Writing in 1972, Deleuze and Guattari were criticizing Samir Amin, the Third World Marxist economist who urged countries in the developing world "to withdraw from the world market." And only three years later (1975), Amin's autarkic policies were in fact adopted by the Khmer Rouge, with calamitous consequences. I do not mean to blame Amin himself, or his theories, for the Khmer Rouge's crimes, as many right-wing commentators have done. But this history does provide a rationale for Deleuze and Guattari's position, as well as showing that they are not just urging a violent acceleration of the market for its own sake. Of course, it should also be noted that, in subsequent decades (from the 1980s onward), the wholehearted adoption of neoliberal policies by developing nations in the global South (often under pressure by the World Bank and the WTO) has also led to calamitous consequences: economic stagnation and widespread immiseration.

In any case, the emphasis on capitalism's destructive, deterritorializing force is picked up in the 1990s by the British philosopher Nick Land. In a series of incendiary essays, Land celebrates absolute deterritorialization as liberation—even (or above all) to the point of total disintegration and death. He simply ignores the reactive side of capitalism in Deleuze and Guattari's account: the side that blocks its own liberatory potentials by operating a "violent and artificial reterritorialization." Instead, Land develops a kind of Stockholm Syndrome with regard to Capital. He sees its absolute, violently destructive speed as an alien force that should be welcomed and celebrated. "What appears to humanity as the history of capitalism is an invasion from the future by an artificial intelligent space that must assemble itself entirely from its enemy's resources." Marxists denounce capitalism for being inhuman and destructive; traditional defenders of capitalism deny these charges outright. Land, however, jams the circuits by rejecting both sides of the binary; he extols capitalism precisely for its inhuman, violent, and destructive power.

Land's position has resonances with that of the early twentieth-century Austrian economist Joseph Schumpeter. Today, Schumpeter is famous for his theory of "creative destruction"—cited by Konstantinou because it is so central to neoliberal ideology. But in fact, the very idea of "creative destruction" comes entirely from Marx. Schumpeter is the only significant right-wing, procapitalist economist who actually took the trouble to read Marx carefully and seriously. And Schumpeter closely follows the *Communist Manifesto* when he highlights the way that capitalism "incessantly revolutionizes the economic structure *from within*." Schumpeter—like a smarter version of Ayn Rand—celebrates the mythical figure of the heroic entrepreneur. Where Marx emphasizes capitalism's long-term tendency toward stagnation, Schumpeter hopes that the entrepreneur's vital innovations can rescue capitalism from its otherwise fatal entropic tendencies. Fifty years later, Land updates Schumpeter's myth in postmodern and posthuman terms with his vision "of a cyberpositively escalating technovirus, of the planetary technological singularity: a self-organizing insidious traumatism, virtually guiding the entire biological desiring-complex towards post-carbon replicator usurpation." Here the entrepreneur is replaced by an entirely nonhuman entity: Capital itself as a viral source of new vitality. Both Schumpeter and Land are writing a sort of accelerationist, antihumanist science fiction. But their stories do not include the final Marxist twist of the negation of the negation, or the expropriation of the expropriators. Instead, Schumpeter's and Land's extrapolations work to theorize the sort of accelerationism that was actually put into practice by Ronald Reagan, Margaret Thatcher, and Deng Xiaoping—and that continues to be maintained by all their successors.

The question remains as to whether accelerationism can

be anything more than the "virulent nihilism" exemplified by Land in theory, and by Thatcher, Reagan, and Deng in practice. Does intensifying the contradictions of capitalism only lead to greater misery and oppression? Or can it also lead to some sort of rupture and affirmative mutation? Is there a way that, as Deleuze once put it, "the techniques of social alienation" can be "reversed into revolutionary means of exploration"? Can we truly start from the bad new things instead of the good old ones?

Alex Williams and Nick Srnicek attempt precisely this in their *Manifesto for an Accelerationist Politics*. They call for a new left politics that is "at ease with a modernity of abstraction, complexity, globality, and technology." Williams and Srnicek seek not to embrace the violent excesses and contradictions of high-technology, neoliberal capitalism but rather to capture this capitalism's most advanced and intensive technologies, so that these technologies can be "*repurposed*" towards common ends. The existing infrastructure is not a capitalist stage to be smashed, but a springboard to launch towards post-capitalism."

Such a project is exemplified, perhaps, in Fredric Jameson's scandalous analysis of the hidden utopian dimension of Wal-Mart. The super-retailer's hyperefficient global organization of product distribution, Jameson says, is something that a future communist society might well wish to make use of. Wal-Mart continually revolutionizes its technologies; it makes use of the latest developments in computation and communications in order to boost productivity and thereby increase its profits. But under different economic conditions, such technologies could just as well be used—and indeed, something like them would *have to be used*—in order to free people as much as possible from meaningless toil. Phenomena like Wal-Mart must be understood dialectically, Jameson tells us, rather than moralistically denounced.

Williams and Srnicek follow this line of thought, as they seek to "unleash latent productive forces" and to "accelerate the process of technological evolution." They reject the idea that the new digital technologies are unavoidably expressive of neoliberal values, but they also reject the "naive" opposing view that technologies are therefore value-free and neutral. They claim, rather, that these technologies are *not exhausted by* the goals under which they have been initially developed, and for which they are currently used. Rather, "given the enslavement of technoscience to capitalist objectives . . . we surely do not yet know what a modern technosocial body can do. Who amongst us fully recognizes what untapped potentials await in the technology which has already been developed?"

I think that this stance is justified, precisely because, as Marshall McLuhan suggests, new media (or, more generally, new technologies) always far exceed their original premises and uses. Stanley Cavell, in his discussion of film, similarly gives a new (postmodern?) twist to the standard modernist claim that the goal of any art is to explore and express the fundamental properties of its medium. What Cavell adds to this traditional account is that "the aesthetic possibilities of a medium are not givens . . . Only the art itself can discover its possibilities, and the discovery of a new possibility is the discovery of a new medium." There is no preexisting "possibility space" for any medium—or, more generally, for any technology. The development and deployment of a technology generates its own affordances and constraints, which themselves may differ under different economic and social conditions.

Technological development will always have a speculative (and nonutilitarian) dimension.

But for this very reason, I am also uneasy with the way that Williams and Srnicek advocate "a Promethean politics of maximal mastery over society and its environment." It is precisely because of the autonomy of technical and material movements from the purposes for which they are initially deployed that these movements are not restricted to their capitalist uses. But this same autonomy puts limits on any hopes of "maximal mastery." Because of what Keynes called radical uncertainty, there are limits to what concerted action can accomplish. We should not expect too much from Promethean foresight, or from the planning and "economic modelling" advocated by Williams and Srnicek.

There has been some confusion on this issue, because Keynesian uncertainty is often wrongly equated with the right-wing doctrine of "unintended consequences." For Hayek and other "free-market" thinkers, any form of planning or intentional action will go astray, thanks to unforeseeable and unintended consequences of these actions. But Hayek claims that the *catallaxy* (spontaneous order) of the market—a twentieth-century update of Adam Smith's "invisible hand"—is somehow miraculously free from such distortions. The market supposedly collates, and therefore "knows," all the available information from all individual economic actors. Prices are "signals" that channel economic activity in an optimal manner. All new events are quickly reflected by changes in prices.

But Hayek's market utopia does not take Keynesian uncertainty into account. Since we cannot quantify the future in probabilistic terms, it cannot be captured in terms of the "information" provided by the price system. Despite its supposedly self-correcting mechanisms, the "market" is as subject to unanticipated consequences and inefficient, disequilibrating outcomes as any planning mechanism would be. We should therefore reject the entire dichotomy between central planning, on the one hand, and market "rationality" on the other. Neither mechanism is guaranteed to produce desirable (or efficient) outcomes; neither is likely to reach any sort of equilibrium; both are subject to shocks and ruptures that cannot be contained within probabilistic calculations of risk.

And in point of fact, despite Hayek's idealization of the market, no corporation actually works by responding to the "information" conveyed in price signals. Rather, capitalist firms themselves engage in massive central planning, in order to manipulate supply, demand, and profit. In other words, planning will take place in any case. It is never as efficacious as the planners wish, but neither is it as futile and ineffective as Hayek claims. The real problem, given the actuality of planning, is to ensure that it is done democratically and accountably, rather than (as at present) by managers and plutocrats accountable only to their corporation's bottom line. But even at best, such planning cannot be foolproof. Williams and Srnicek simply invert Hayek's dichotomy between planning and emergent order, when the dichotomy as such needs to be abandoned.

Marx famously says that "men [sic] make their own history, but they do not make it as they please; they do not make it under self-selected circumstances, but under circumstances existing already, given and transmitted from the past." This will remain the case under a postcapitalist economic system. Even as we pass over from the "realm of necessity" to the "realm of freedom," the field of human endeavor will not be limitless. It will still be constrained by previous social, physical, and environmental conditions, by what Whitehead calls "stubborn fact which cannot be evaded." Even if capitalist crisis *does* eventually open the doors to new and better social relations (as Marx hoped), instead of just allowing the system to perpetuate itself indefinitely (as seems to be the case today), the traces of the contradictions that precipitated the crisis will remain. Hegel was never more wrong than when he claimed that "the wounds of the Spirit heal, and leave no scars behind."

In particular, the affordances offered by new technologies are not limited to their current, consciously intended uses under capitalism; but they are also not entirely flexible. For our tools incessantly modify us, even as we produce and extend them. We cannot simply manipulate them just as we please. This means that we need to engage in *alliances* with our tools, as Bruno Latour would say, rather than seeing them as flawless instruments or prosthetic extensions of our will.

This brings us back to the ambivalence at the heart of accelerationism. Speculative extrapolation comes without guarantees. When we push potentialities to their fullest expression, or exacerbate contradictions to the point where they explode, we cannot be sure what the outcome will be. We face fundamental uncertainty, and not just calculable risk. Deleuze and Guattari, following Marx, insist that "the real barrier of capitalist production is capital itself." This means that we live in a regime of "real subsumption," where all potentials for change are immanently contained within the relational field of Capital itself. Accelerationism may just as well result in the horrific intensification of "actually existing" capitalist relations (Land), as in the radical displacement and transmutation of these relations (Williams and Srnicek). This is why accelerationism needs to be an aesthetic program first, before it can be a political one. Speculative fiction can explore the abyss of accelerationist ambivalence, without prematurely pretending to resolve it.

Richard K. Morgan's near-future thriller *Market Forces* is an exemplary accelerationist fiction. It envisions a world in which the corporate practices of the present have pushed to their logical culmination. In the world of the novel, the vast majority of the population lives in violence-ridden squalor behind barbed-wire fences, sequestered in "cordoned zones." Meanwhile, members of the corporate elite—the only people still able to afford automobiles and gasoline—compete for contracts and promotions through *Mad Max*–style road rage duels to the death. For it is simply "realistic"—a "hard-edged solution for hard-edged times"—to make life-and-death decisions that can only be enforced through competitive struggle. Under the harsh discipline of the market, morals are an unaffordable luxury. Even the slightest weakness or hesitation is immediately punished. As one character memorably puts it: "I'd say a practicing free market economist has blood on his hands, or he isn't doing his job properly. It comes with the market, and the decisions it demands. Hard decisions, decisions of life and death."

This utterance has a kind of blunt, empirical directness, as if to say: "I'm giving it to you straight, no alibis, no evasions. It may not look pretty, but the world is a harsh and cruel place. Tough decisions—pragmatic and realistic, free of illusions—have to be made, one way or another. If you don't have blood on your hands, you are just an ineffectual dreamer, out of touch with the world as it actually is." I think this is a tone that we are all familiar with; we hear it often, coming from politicians and financiers alike. Neoliberal logic is perfectly expressed in Morgan's novel, with the rhetoric ramped up only a little bit: the appeal to a hard-nosed "realism," the contemptuous dismissal of idle dreams, the cynical justification of rapaciousness as sheer necessity.

Market Forces simply takes at its word the neoliberal dogma that "there is no alternative" to globalized capitalism and that vigorous market competition is the best way to resolve all problems. In the seventeenth century, Thomas Hobbes argued that a strong State was needed in order to suppress an otherwise unending "war of all against all." But in the twenty-first century, Morgan suggests, our policy is very nearly the reverse. Now, the important thing is to incite and promote competition, to make sure that a "war of all against all" takes place, no matter what. As Foucault similarly puts it, for today's neoliberalism, "competition is not a primitive given"; rather, it is an ideal, a desideratum: something that has to be "carefully and artificially constructed" through a series of "lengthy efforts." In the terms of Morgan's novel, we always need to impose "conflict incentives," in order to force people to perform at their highest potential.

In the world of *Market Forces*, the hottest field in finance is Conflict Investment, which means funding civil wars and rebellions in "developing" countries, in return for extravagant profits (from kickbacks, interest payments, and the control of factories in tax-free "enterprise zones") if the side you are backing wins. The rationale for this is entirely market-based. "Human beings have been fighting wars as long as history recalls," a finance executive tells us.

> "It is in our nature, it is in our genes. In the last half of the last century the peacemakers, the *governments* of this world, did not

end war. They simply *managed* it, and they managed it *badly*. They poured money, without thought of return, into conflicts and guerrilla armies abroad . . . They were partisan, dogmatic, and inefficient. Billions wasted in poorly assessed wars that no sane investor would have looked at twice.

"But what governments did poorly, the market can do better. When faced with a rebellion in a poor country, a Conflict Investment manager says, "we are concerned with only two things. Will they win? And will it pay? . . . We do not judge. We do not moralize. We do not waste. Instead, we assess, we invest. And we prosper."

Market Forces does not offer us a way out from capitalist realism. One of Morgan's other science fiction novels, *Woken Furies*, in fact, considers at great length the possibilities for a democratic, egalitarian socialist revolution in a corporate-dominated society much like our own. But *Market Forces* just explores the extreme ramifications of the neoliberal order, giving us no distance or respite. It's as if Morgan were saying to the reader, "I'm going to subject you to the worst; I will throw the most violently oppressive social conditions, and the most horrific and disgusting incidents, in your face, and see if you are tough enough to take it." (Perhaps I should write "man enough," instead of "tough enough," since Morgan insists on the male supremacism that underlies the neoliberal order.) This is accelerationism at its purest—without Williams and Srnicek's hopes for escape or redemption, but also without anything like Land's apologia-in-the-guise-of-apocalyptic-vision.

The novel ends, rather like a Kurt Russell movie, with its protagonist, Chris Faulkner, as the last man standing—or, more precisely, driving—after having killed off all his rivals. "I can do whatever the fuck I want," Chris says; "men like me, there's nothing you can do to stop us anymore." But Morgan deliberately empties out this action-movie cliché, even as he repeats it. For all of Chris's macho accomplishment, he is little more than the power of capital accumulation personified; in a world devastated by that relentless accumulation, there is nothing that he can do except "[give] himself up to the snarl of the engine, the spreading numbness of the drugs in his system, and the onrushing emptiness of the road ahead."

Accelerationist Aesthetics

TOUT SE RÉSUME *dans l'Esthétique et l'Économie politique.*
Everything comes down to Aesthetics and Political Economy.
Mallarmé's aphorism is my starting point for considering
accelerationist aesthetics. I think that aesthetics exists in a
special relationship to political economy, precisely because
aesthetics is the one thing that cannot be reduced to political
economy. Politics, ethics, epistemology, and even ontology are
all subject to "determination in the last instance" by the forces
and relations of production. On a human scale, this is Marx's
central thesis; but it also holds true on a cosmic scale, where
the determining forces and relations are those described by
subatomic physics and thermodynamics. Aesthetics is the
lone exception to this rule; it does not violate the "laws" of
political and physical economy, but it oddly subsists alongside
these economies and apart from them. There is something
spectral, and curiously insubstantial, about aesthetics; its
action is not direct, but *vicarious*. In its own oblique and qua-
si-primordial way, "aesthetics becomes first philosophy"—as
Graham Harman puts it. Aesthetics is never essential, but
this is what allows it to be irreducible to the essential.

Kant says two important things about what he calls aesthetic judgment. The first is that any such judgment is necessarily "disinterested." This means that it doesn't relate to my own needs and desires. It is something that I enjoy entirely for its own sake, with no ulterior motives, and with no profit to myself. When I find something to be beautiful, I am "indifferent" to any uses that thing might have; I am even indifferent to whether the thing in question actually exists or not. This is why aesthetic sensation is the one realm of existence that is not reducible to political economy.

Of course, this doesn't mean that I am actually liberated by art from worldly concerns. The constraints of political economy can, and do, get in the way of aesthetics. A starving person is blocked from full aesthetic enjoyment. It is only when I am well fed—"only when the need" arising from hunger "is satisfied"—that I enjoy delicacies of cuisine. And it is only "as long as we find ourselves in safety" that we can enjoy sublime spectacles of danger. Beauty in itself is inefficacious. But this also means that beauty is in and of itself utopian. For beauty presupposes a liberation from need; it offers us a way out from the artificial scarcity imposed by the capitalist mode of production. However, since we do in fact live under this mode of production, beauty is only a "promise of happiness" (as Stendhal said) rather than happiness itself. Aesthetics, for us, is unavoidably fleeting and spectral. When time is money and labor is 24/7, we don't have the *luxury* to be indifferent to anything's existence. To use a distinction made by Michael Moorcock and China Miéville, art under capitalism at best offers us escapism, rather than the actual prospect of escape.

The second important thing that Kant says about aesthetic judgment is that "it is not a cognitive judgment," for "it is in itself indeterminable and unfit for cognition." This means that beauty cannot be subsumed under any concept. An aesthetic judgment is therefore singular and ungrounded. Aesthetic experience has nothing to do with "information" or "facts." It cannot be generalized, or transformed into any sort of positive knowledge. How could it, when it doesn't serve any function or purpose beyond itself? And this, again, is why aesthetic sensation seems spectral to us, and even epiphenomenal. It cannot be extracted, appropriated, or put to work.

Analytic philosophers of mind, frustrated by this impossibility, have spent decades trying to argue that aesthetic experience—or what they more often call inner sensation, or the experience of "qualia," or "consciousness" *tout court*—doesn't really exist. As Wittgenstein famously phrased it: "a wheel that can be turned though nothing else moves with it, is not part of the mechanism." Later thinkers have transformed Wittgenstein's puzzlement about inner experience into dogmatic denial that it can be anything other than an illusion. But the basic point still stands. Aesthetics marks the strange persistence of what (to quote Wittgenstein again) "is not a *something*, but not a *nothing* either!" Aesthetic experience is not part of any cognitive mechanism—even though it is never encountered *apart from* such a mechanism.

What is the role of aesthetics, then, today? I said that beauty cannot be subsumed; yet we live in a time when financial mechanisms subsume everything there is. Capitalism has moved from "formal subsumption" to "real subsumption." These terms, originally coined in passing by Marx, have been taken up and elaborated by thinkers in the Italian Autonomist tradition, most notably Michael Hardt and Antonio Negri. For Marx, it is *labor* that is "subsumed" under capital. In formal subsumption, capital appropriates, and extracts a surplus from, labor processes that precede capitalism, or that at the very least are not organized by capitalism. In real subsumption, there is no longer any such autonomy; labor itself is directly organized in capitalist terms (think of the factory and the assembly line).

In Hardt and Negri's expanded redefinition of "subsumption," it isn't just labor that is subsumed by capital, but all aspects of personal and social life. This means that everything in life must now be seen as a kind of labor: we are still working even when we consume and even when we are asleep. Affects and feelings, linguistic abilities, modes of cooperation, forms of know-how and of explicit knowledge, expressions of desire: all these are appropriated and turned into sources of surplus value. We have moved from a situation of extrinsic exploitation, in which capital subordinated labor and subjectivity to its purposes, to a situation of intrinsic exploitation, in which capital directly incorporates labor and subjectivity *within* its own processes.

This means that labor, subjectivity, and social life are no longer "outside" capital and antagonistic to it. Rather, they are immediately produced as parts of it. They cannot resist the depredations of capital, because they are themselves already functions of capital. This is what leads us to speak of such things as "social capital," "cultural capital," and "human capital": as if our knowledge, our abilities, our beliefs, and our desires had only instrumental value and needed to be invested. Everything we live and do, everything we experience, is quickly reduced to the status of "dead labour, that, vampire-like, only lives by sucking living labour, and lives the more, the more labour it sucks." Under a regime of real subsumption, every living person is transformed into a capital stock that must not lie fallow but has to be profitably invested. The individual is assumed—and indeed compelled—to be, as Foucault puts it, "an entrepreneur, an entrepreneur of himself . . . being for himself his own capital, being for himself his own producer, being for himself the source of [his] earnings."

This process of real subsumption is the key to our globalized network society. Everything without exception is subordinated to an economic logic, an economic rationality. Everything must be measured, and made commensurable, through the mediation of some sort of "universal equivalent": money or information. Real subsumption is facilitated by— but also provides the impetus for—the revolutionization of computing and communication technologies over the course of the past several decades. Today we live in a digital world, a world of financial derivatives and big data. Virtual reality supplements and enhances physical, "face-to-face" reality, rather than being, as we used to naively think, opposed to it. Neoliberalism is not just the ideology or belief system of this form of capitalism. It is also, more importantly, the concrete way in which the system works. It is an actual set of practices and institutions. It provides both a calculus for judging human actions and a mechanism for inciting and directing those actions.

What does this mean for aesthetics? The process of real subsumption requires the valuation and evaluation of everything, even of that which is spectral, epiphenomenal, and without value. Real subsumption leaves no aspect of life uncolonized. It endeavors to capture and to put to work even those things that are uneconomical, or "not part of the mechanism." Affect and inner experience are not exempt from this process of subsumption, appropriation, and extraction of a surplus. For capitalism now seeks to expropriate surplus value not just from labor narrowly considered but from leisure as well, not just from "private property" but also from what the

Autonomists call "the common," and not just from palpable things but also from feelings and moods and subjective states. Everything must be marketed and made subject to competition. Everything must be identified as a "brand."

This leads to a veritable Kantian Antinomy of the aesthetic under late capitalism. Aesthetics must be simultaneously promoted beyond all measure, and yet reduced to nothing. On the one hand, as Fredric Jameson noted long ago:

> Aesthetic production today has become integrated into commodity production generally: the frantic economic urgency of producing fresh waves of ever more novel-seeming goods (from clothing to airplanes), at ever greater rates of turnover, now assigns an increasingly essential structural function and position to aesthetic innovation and experimentation.

Or as the free-market economist Virginia Postrel cheerily and uncritically puts the same argument, "aesthetics, or styling, has become an accepted unique selling point, on a global basis." In today's capitalism *everything* is aestheticized, and all values are ultimately aesthetic ones.

Yet at the same time, this ubiquitous aestheticization is also a radical extirpation of the aesthetic. It's not just that sensations and feelings are trivialized when they are packaged for sale and indexed upon the most minute variations of product lines; it's also that the two most crucial qualities of the aesthetic according to Kant—that it is disinterested and that it is noncognitive—are made to vanish or are explained away. Aesthetic sensations and feelings are no longer disinterested, because they have been recast as markers of personal identity: revealed preferences, brands, lifestyle markers, objects of adoration by fans. Aesthetic sensations and feelings are also ruthlessly cognized: for it is only insofar as they are known and objectively described, or transformed into data, that they can be exploited as forms of labor and marketed as fresh experiences and exciting lifestyle choices. Ironically, then, it is precisely in a time when the "affective labor" is privileged over material production, and when marketing is increasingly concerned with impalpable commodities like moods, experiences, and "atmospheres," that we enter into the regime of a fully "cognitive capitalism," guided by the findings of cognitive psychology and cognitive philosophy of mind.

It is under the conditions of real subsumption that accelerationism first becomes a possible aesthetic strategy. It is a fairly recent invention. In the twentieth century, before the developments that I have recounted, the most vibrant art was all about transgression. Modernist artists sought to shatter taboos, to scandalize audiences, and to pass beyond the limits of bourgeois "good taste." From Stravinsky to the Dadaists, from Bataille to the makers of *Deep Throat*, and from Charlie Parker to Elvis to Guns N' Roses, the aim was always to stun audiences, by pushing things further than they had ever been pushed before. Offensiveness was a measure of success. Transgression was simply and axiomatically taken to be subversive.

But this is no longer the case today. Neoliberalism has no problem with excess. Far from being subversive, transgression today is entirely normative. Nobody is really offended by Marilyn Manson or Quentin Tarantino. Every supposedly "transgressive" act or representation expands the field of capital investment. It opens up new territories to appropriate, and jump-starts new processes from which to extract surplus value. What else could happen, at a time when leisure and enjoyment have themselves become forms of labor? Business and marketing practices today are increasingly focused upon novelty and innovation. More rapid turnover is one way to combat what Marx called the tendential fall of the rate of profit. Far from being subversive or oppositional, transgression is the actual motor of capitalist expansion today: the way that it renews itself in orgies of "creative destruction."

In other words, political economy today is driven by resonating loops of positive feedback. Finance operates according to a transgressive cultural logic of manic innovation and ever-ramifying metalevels of self-referential abstraction. This easily reaches the point where financial derivatives, for instance, float in a hyperspace of pure contingency, free of indexical relation, as Elie Ayache shows, to any "underlying" whatsoever. At the same time that it floats off into digital abstraction, however, neoliberalism also operates directly on our bodies. Data are extracted from everything that we feel and think do. These data are appropriated and consolidated, and then packaged and sold back to us.

In such a climate, nothing is more prized than excess. The further out you go, the more there is to accumulate and capitalize upon. Everything is organized in terms of thresholds, intensities, and modulations. As Robin James puts it, "for the neoliberal subject, the point of life is to 'push it to the limit,' closing in ever more narrowly on the point of diminishing returns . . . The neoliberal subject has an insatiable appetite for more and more novel differences." The point is always to reach "the edge of burnout": to pursue a line of intensification and yet to be able to pull back from this edge, treating it as an investment and recuperating the intensity as profit. As James says, "privileged people get to lead the most intense lives, lives of maximized (individual and social) investment and maximized return."

This is why transgression no longer works as a subversive

aesthetic strategy. Or more precisely, transgression works *all too well* as a strategy for amassing both "cultural capital" and actual capital, and thereby it misses what I have been calling the spectrality and epiphenomenality of the aesthetic. Transgression is now fully incorporated into the logic of political economy. It testifies to the way that, as Hardt and Negri say, under the regime of real subsumption, "there is nothing, no 'naked life,' no external standpoint . . . there is no longer an 'outside' to power." Where transgressive modernist art sought to break free from social constraints, and thereby to attain some radical Outside, accelerationist art remains entirely immanent, modulating its intensities in place. As James says, in neoliberal art "life's intensity, like a sine wave, closes in on a limit without ever reaching it."

The deadlock of accelerationism as a political strategy has much to do with the aesthetic failure of transgression. They are really two sides of the same process. The acceleration of capitalism itself in the decades since 1980 has become a classic example of how we must be careful what we wish for—because we just might get it. As a result of the neoliberal "reforms" of the past thirty-five years or so, the full savagery of capitalism has been unleashed, no longer held back by the checks and balances of financial regulation and social welfare. At the same time, what Boltanski and Chiapello call the "new spirit of capitalism" successfully took up the subjective demands of the 1960s and 1970s and made them its own. Neoliberalism now offers us things like personal autonomy, sexual freedom, and individual "self-realization"; though of course, these often take on the sinister form of precarity, insecurity, and continual pressure to perform. Neoliberal capitalism today lures us with the prospect of living, in James's words, "the most intense lives, lives of maximized (individual and social) investment and maximized return," while at the same time it privatizes, expropriates, and extracts a surplus from everything in sight.

In other words, the problem with accelerationism as a political strategy has to do with the fact that—like it or not—we are all accelerationists now. It has become increasingly clear that crises and contradictions do not lead to the demise of capitalism. Rather, they actually work to promote and advance capitalism, by providing it with its fuel. Crises do not endanger the capitalist order; rather, they are occasions for the dramas of "creative destruction" by means of which, phoenix-like, capitalism repeatedly renews itself. We are all caught within this loop. And accelerationism in philosophy or political economy offers us, at best, an exacerbated awareness of how we are trapped.

By all accounts, the situation is far worse today than it was in the 1990s, let alone the 1970s. Indeed, we have moved with alarming rapidity from the neoliberal triumphalism of the 1990s to our current sense—in the wake of the financial collapse of 2008—that neoliberalism is entirely defunct as an ideology. Unfortunately, the intellectual discredit into which it has fallen does not impede its functioning in the slightest. Its programs and processes remain in full force; if anything, they are being pushed further than ever at the present moment. The zombie system under which we live refuses to die, no matter how oppressive and dysfunctional it is.

In this situation, what can it mean to propose an accelerationist aesthetic? Can it turn out any differently than transgression? Can it offer us anything other, or anything more, than the actually existing accelerationism of our politico-economic condition? The aesthetic case for accelerationism is perhaps best expressed by something that Deleuze wrote in an entirely different context:

> It often happens that Nietzsche comes face to face with something sickening, ignoble, disgusting. Well, Nietzsche thinks it's funny, and he would add fuel to the fire if he could. He says: keep going, it's still not disgusting enough. Or he says: excellent, how disgusting, what a marvel, what a masterpiece, a poisonous flower, finally the "human species is getting interesting."

I do not think that this is an accurate evocation of Nietzsche. For Nietzsche does not really have this sort of attitude toward what he sees as the "decadent" bourgeois culture of his own time. Rather, Nietzsche is most often overwhelmed with disgust at what he sees of the world around him. His epic struggle against his own disgust, and his heroic efforts to overcome it, are at the center of *Thus Spoke Zarathustra*. The shrill and stridently repetitious tone of Nietzsche's praise of cheerfulness and laughter indicates that these attitudes did not come easily to him. Nor does he tend to adopt them when confronted with the "sickening, ignoble, disgusting" spectacles of his own culture and society.

Nonetheless, I think that the attitude described by Deleuze is a good fit for accelerationist art today. Intensifying the horrors of contemporary capitalism does not lead them to explode, but it does offer us a kind of satisfaction and relief, by telling us that we have finally hit bottom, finally realized the worst. This is what really animates recent accelerationist works—such as, for instance, Mark Neveldine and Brian Taylor's exploitation movie *Gamer*. These works may be critical, but they also revel in the sleaze and exploitation that they so eagerly put on display. Thanks to their enlightened cynicism—their finding all these "sickening, ignoble, disgusting" conditions funny—they do not offer us the false hope that piling on the worst that neoliberal capitalism has to offer will somehow help to lead us beyond it. These works may be *excessive*, but—as Robin James observes—under the conditions of neoliberalism "excess doesn't negate or reject, but *overdrives normal, everyday life-and-death reality.*"

Peter Watts's short story "Hotshot" offers us a similar sort of bleak humor. The story's narrator and protagonist, Sunday Ahzmundin, is trying to decide whether to join an expedition to colonize another star system. She doesn't really want to commit herself to a flight lasting thousands of years, most of it spent in suspended animation. But she cannot really stay behind either, given the conditions back on Earth: "the dust zones, the drowned coastlines, the weedy impoverished ecosystems choking to death on centuries of human effluent." In a throwaway line, Sunday mentions watching "archival video of the Koch lynchings, which made us feel a little better but didn't really change anything."

The reference is presumably to the billionaire brothers Charles G. Koch and David H. Koch, owners of the privately held Koch Industries. The company is heavily involved in petroleum production. The brothers themselves are best known for their massive political spending, much of it in opposition to environmental regulation and climate-change legislation. They have also led initiatives against public transportation and against the use of solar power as an alternative energy source. The Koch brothers could be considered accelerationists of a sort; it almost seems as if, under the cloak of climate denialism, they were deliberately trying to increase CO_2 emissions and to raise the average global temperature as high as possible.

36

Watts places the "Koch lynchings" in a *future anterior*. That is to say, in the present time of his story—which is narrated in the present tense—the killings have already happened. The Koch brothers, we are told, were punished for their role in making human life on Earth unsustainable. The word "lynching" has ugly connotations; even at best, it suggests spontaneous action, without taking the trouble to observe legal norms. The presence of "archival video" suggests that the killings were not done quietly and privately, but were broadcast to a worldwide audience. Presumably the killings provided relief for billions of people (they "made us feel a little better"), because they satisfied a basic desire: to punish those responsible for wantonly destroying our future. As Watts has written elsewhere, "ethics and morality are not human traits; they're *mammalian* ones . . . Any number of social species have what you might call a *justice instinct*: a drive to punish cheaters and freeloaders."

But I think that this "justice instinct" is more an aesthetic urge than an ethical one. Lynching the Koch brothers would be satisfying in itself, regardless of any purpose that it might serve. And indeed, Sunny tells us that the killings "didn't really change anything." By the time the perpetrators are put to death, the damage has already been done. Global warming is a long-term process; even if we reduced carbon emissions to zero, starting today, the planet would continue to heat up for several more decades. In the end, the Koch lynchings in Watts's story are too little, too late. At best, they provide a gloss on a situation that is already irreparable. Such is the dilemma of aesthetic accelerationism.

Paolo Bacigalupi's short story "The People of Sand and Slag" also provides a post-hoc vision of ecological catastrophe. The narrator, and the other two members of his crew, are posthumans, genetically engineered and augmented in radical ways. They have "transcended the animal kingdom." But if their bodies and minds make them into Promethean beings, this is only ironically. For their alterations from the human baseline testify, not so much to "maximal mastery" as to the harsh demands of a radically changed, unforgiving environment. These posthumans are soldiers, guarding an automated mining operation in Montana. The three of them share a close *esprit de corps*; otherwise, they seem devoid of empathy or compassion. As befits their job, they are extremely strong and fast; when they are hurt, their wounds heal quickly and easily. Sometimes, during sex play or just for fun, they embed razors and knives in their skin, or even chop off their own limbs; everything heals, or grows back, in less than a day. For food, they consume sand, petroleum, mining leftovers, and other industrial waste. They live and work in what for us would be a hellish landscape of "acid pits and tailings mountains," and other residues of scorched-earth strip mining. And for vacation, they go off to Hawaii, and swim in the oil-slick-laden, plastic-strewn Pacific. They seem perfectly adapted to their environment, a world in which nearly all unengineered life forms have gone extinct and in which corporate competition apparently takes the form of incessant low-grade armed conflict.

In the course of Bacigalupi's story, the soldier protagonists come upon a dog. The creature is almost entirely unknown to them; they have never seen one before, except in zoos or on the Web. Nobody can explain where the dog came from or how it survived in a place that was toxic to it and that had none of its usual food sources. The soldiers keep the dog for a while, as a curiosity. They do not understand how it could ever have survived, even in an unpolluted and pre–biologically engineered world. They take for granted that it is "not sentient," and they are surprised when it shows affection for them and when they discover that it can be taught to obey simple commands.

The soldiers are perturbed by just how "vulnerable" the dog is. In this post-Anthropocene climate, it needs special food and water, and incessant care. They find that they continually "have to worry about whether it was going to step in acid, or tangle in barb-wire half-buried in the sand, or eat something that would keep it up vomiting half the night." In this world, a dog is "very expensive to maintain . . . Manufacturing a basic organism's food is quite complex . . . Recreating the web of life isn't easy." In the end, it's simply too much annoyance and expense to keep the dog around. So the soldiers kill it, cook it over a spit, and eat it. Though they have been told that dog meat used to be a culinary delicacy, they do not find it to be anywhere near as tasty as their usual diet of petroleum and sand: "it tasted okay, but in the end it was hard to understand the big deal."

Aesthetic accelerationism, unlike the politico-economic kind, does not claim any efficacy for its own operations. It revels in depicting situations where the worst depredations of capitalism have come to pass, and where people are not only unable to change things but are even unable to imagine trying to change things. This is capitalist realism in full effect. Aesthetic accelerationism does not even deny that its own intensities serve the aim of extracting surplus value and accumulating profit. The evident complicity and bad faith of these works, their reveling in the base passions that Nietzsche disdained, and their refusal to sustain outrage or claim the moral high ground: all these postures help to move us toward the disinterest and epiphenomenality of the aesthetic. So I don't make any political claims for this sort of accelerationist art—indeed, I would undermine my whole argument were I to do so. But I do want to claim a certain *aesthetic inefficacy* for them—which is something that works of transgression and negativity cannot hope to attain today.

Parasites on the Body
of Capital

BENJAMIN NOYS, who actually coined the term *acceleration-ism*, defines it as "an exotic variant of *la politique du pire*: if capitalism generates its own forces of dissolution then the necessity is to radicalise capitalism itself: the worse the better." But perhaps Noys's critique is a bit unfair. Accelerationism is a new response to the specific conditions of today's neoliberal, globalized and networked, capitalism. But it is solidly rooted in traditional Marxist thought. Marx himself writes both of capitalism's revolutionary effects and of the contradictions that render it unviable. In the *Communist Manifesto*, Marx and Engels write that capitalism is characterized thus:

> Constant revolutionizing of production, uninterrupted distur-bance of all social conditions, everlasting uncertainty and agita-tion distinguish the bourgeois epoch from all earlier ones. All fixed, fast-frozen relations, with their train of ancient and venera-ble prejudices and opinions, are swept away, all new-formed ones become antiquated before they can ossify. All that is solid melts into air, all that is holy is profaned, and man is at last compelled to face with sober senses his real conditions of life, and his relations with his kind.

Note how, in this passage, capitalism's relentless "revolution-izing" of technologies and social relations also revolutionizes our self-understanding. As capitalism shakes up the material basis of life, it also demystifies and disenchants; it destroys all of the old mythical explanations and legitimations that were previously used to justify our place in society, and in the cosmos. And this destruction has only gone further in the years since Marx and Engels wrote. What Max Weber, somewhat later, called the "disenchantment of the world" has proceeded by leaps and bounds in the twentieth and twen-ty-first centuries. While all those "ancient and venerable prej-udices and opinions" are still quite vehemently held, they have lost their grounding and their authority. Today we are left, as Ray Brassier puts it, with a world in which "intelligibility has become detached from meaning."

Weber and Brassier both attribute this disenchantment to the progress of science. Marx would not have disputed such assertions, but he attributes scientific progress itself to capitalism's overwhelming development of productive forces. This does not mean that science is in any sense arbitrary or "socially constructed." But without the requisite social and economic conditions, scientific discovery on the scale that we currently take for granted would not have happened in the first place. This is why Brassier's account, following Sellars, of science as the construction of inferential links in the logical space of reasons is little more than a *post hoc* idealization. Such an account does not tell us very much about *how* science actually works, and it is far too vague and general to serve as an explanation for *why* science works.

In any case, Marx refuses to separate the liberating effects of the "constant revolutionizing of production"—including the accelerated pace of scientific discovery—from its creation

42

of vast human misery. The good and the bad go together. In other words, capitalism is beset by severe internal contradictions. In particular, Marx emphasizes a violent discordance between the *forces of production* unleashed by capitalism and the *relations of production* that organize these forces. Beset by this tension, capitalism has no finality. It cannot be the ultimate horizon of history (or of scientific discovery and technological invention). Rather, Marx insists that the contradiction between forces and relations will lead to capitalism's downfall:

> The monopoly of capital becomes a fetter upon the mode of production which has flourished alongside and under it. The centralization of the means of production and the socialization of labour reach a point at which they become incompatible with their capitalist integument. This integument is burst asunder. The knell of capitalist private property sounds. The expropriators are expropriated.

At the risk of belaboring the obvious, I will point out that Marx's diagnosis of the maladies of capitalism has been amply confirmed by subsequent events. Obviously, though, his vision of a movement beyond capitalism has not come to pass. In today's neoliberal, globalized network society, "the monopoly of capital" has indeed become "a fetter upon the mode of production." We can see this in all sorts of ways. So-called austerity programs transfer ever more wealth to the already rich, at the price of undermining living standards for the population as a whole. The privatization of formerly public services and the expropriation of formerly common resources undermine the very infrastructures that are essential for long-term survival. "Digital rights management" and copy protection restrict the flow of data and cripple the power of the computing technologies that make them possible in the first place.

Ubiquitous surveillance by both corporate and governmental entities, and the consequent consolidation of "Big Data," leads to stultification at precisely those points where neoliberal ideology calls for "flexibility" and "creativity." Investment is increasingly directed toward derivatives and other arcane financial instruments; the more these claim to comprehend the future by pricing "risk," the more thoroughly they move away from any grounding in actual productive activity. And of course, massive environmental deterioration results from the way that actual energetic expenditures are written off by businesses as so-called externalities.

And yet, none of these contradictions have caused the system to collapse or have even remotely menaced its expanded reproduction. As Deleuze and Guattari say, "no one has ever died from contradictions." Instead, capitalism perpetuates itself through a continual series of readjustments. Despite the fact that we have reached a point where capitalist property relations have become an onerous "fetter upon the mode of production" that they initially helped to put into motion, this fetter shows no sign of being lifted. The intensification of capitalism's contradictions has not led to an explosion or to any "negation of the negation." The "capitalist integument" has failed to "burst asunder"; instead, it has calcified into a rigid carapace, well-nigh suffocating the life within.

Marx was perhaps being too faithful to Hegel when he described the tension between forces and relations as a "contradiction"—implying that it could develop into a higher stage by means of a dialectical resolution or supersession. The discordance might be better understood as an insurpassable paradox. The crippling tension between forces of production and relations of production does not ever truly resolve itself but rather reproduces itself on a larger scale each time that it seems to have been overcome. Hegel was wrong; the real is unquestionably *not* rational. We are stuck within the process that Hegel stigmatized as the "bad infinity." Hegelian dialectics is not adequate to describe the delirious, irrational "logic" of capital—even though Marx himself originally analyzed this "logic" by means of Hegelian categories. For our experiences of the past century have taught us that the worse its own internal contradictions get, the more thoroughly capitalism is empowered.

Marx famously writes that "capital is dead labour which, vampire-like, only lives by sucking living labour, and lives the more, the more labour it sucks." But in fact, capital is even more monstrous than this. For it is actively auto-cannibalistic. It feeds not only on living labor but also upon itself. In times of crisis, Marx tells us, we witness "the violent destruction of capital, not by relations external to it, but rather as a condition of its self-preservation." When profit rates decline, then vast conflagrations of value—whether in wars or in economic crises—are necessary in order to allow the accumulation of capital to resume anew. Rather than being undone by its own internal contradictions, capitalism both *needs* and *uses* these contradictions; it continually regenerates itself by means of them, and indeed it could not survive without them. It follows that we cannot hope to *negate* capitalism, because capitalism itself already mobilizes a far greater negativity than anything we could possibly mount against it. This in turn leads us to the paradox that capitalism creates abundance, but at the same time it always needs to transform this abundance into an imposed scarcity. Deleuze and Guattari are right to note that scarcity, or "lack," is not the attribute of some supposed "state of nature"; rather, "lack (*manque*) is created, planned, and organized in and through social production . . . The deliberate creation of lack as a function of market economy is the art of a dominant class," and it ironically takes place "amid an abundance of production."

Capitalism *has to* transform plenitude into scarcity, because it cannot endure its own abundance. Again and again, as Marx and Engels say in the *Manifesto,* under capitalism "there breaks out an epidemic that, in all earlier epochs, would have seemed an absurdity—the epidemic of over-production." The wealth that capitalism actually produces undermines the scarcity that remains its *raison d'etre.* For once scarcity has been overcome, there is nothing left to drive competition. The imperative to expand and intensify production simply becomes absurd. In the face of abundance, therefore, capitalism needs to generate an imposed scarcity, simply in order to keep itself going.

Accelerationism is perhaps best understood as a response to this strange dilemma. It starts from the observation that actually existing capitalism has in fact brought us to the point where—perhaps for the first time in human history—universal affluence is at least conceivable. We live in an age of astonishing scientific discoveries and technological inventions. Computers process information as never before; we are starting to manipulate life itself on the genetic level; we will soon be able to utilize energy from the sun, freeing us from dependence upon the environmentally destructive, and physically limited, stock of fossil fuels. Thanks to advances in automation, there is probably less need for irksome labor today than at any time since before the invention of agriculture. With its globe-spanning technologies, its creation and use of an incredibly powerful computation and communications infrastructure, its mobilization of general intellect, and its machinic automation of irksome toil, contemporary capitalism has already provided us with the *conditions* for universal abundance. We no longer need to wait for some distant future: because, as William Gibson famously put it, "the future is already here—it's just not very evenly distributed."

We should not underestimate the significance of this situation. In our world today, there is *already* enough accumulated wealth, and sufficiently advanced technology, for every human being to lead a life of leisure and self-cultivation. In principle at least (although of course not in practice) we have solved the *economic problem* of humankind—just as John Maynard Keynes, writing in 1930, predicted we would do within a century. Keynes rightly foresees such twenty-first century phenomena as "*technological unemployment*." But he sees these phenomena as opportunities rather than problems: "this means that the economic problem is not—if we look into the future—*the permanent problem of the human race*." Instead, Keynes says,

> for the first time since his creation man will be faced with his real, his permanent problem—how to use his freedom from pressing economic cares, how to occupy the leisure, which science and compound interest will have won for him, to live wisely and agreeably and well.

Keynes's vision of the "economic possibilities for our grandchildren" can be contrasted with Joseph Schumpeter's assertion, made at roughly the same time, that, "in order to identify himself with the capitalist system, the unemployed of today would have completely to forget his personal fate" and instead "comfort himself with hopes for his great-grandchildren." Schumpeter, unlike his twenty-first century acolytes, takes the "destruction" part of "creative destruction" seriously; you don't find him celebrating "disruption" in the self-congratulatory manner of today's management gurus. For Schumpeter, the continual revolutionizing of the means of production also means a continual deferral of our enjoyment of the fruits of that production. But where Schumpeter can only conceive of an endless recession of the moment of prosperity, Keynes regards this prosperity as an actually attainable state.

Keynes's vision of the future can also be contrasted with that of his contemporary and antagonist, the neoliberal philosopher Friedrich Hayek. Keynes's biographer, Robert Skidelsky, compares the two at great length. He notes that both thinkers are concerned with how "liberalism could most successfully be defended" in face of the shocks of the first half of the twentieth century. Keynes and Hayek both seek, in other words, to rescue capitalism, but where "Hayek was a fervent, consistent believer in the virtues of capitalism; Keynes's belief was certainly not fervent, and perhaps only intermittent." Keynes sees capital accumulation as only a means; "compound interest" is a tool to lead us to lives of leisure. For Hayek, in contrast, "the end-state cannot be distinguished from the processes which generate it"; the "economic problem" must remain humankind's permanent one. In Hayek's vision, there is "no life beyond capitalism, no knowledge of the good life beyond the discovery process of the market." And this remains a core principle of neoliberalism today. Hayek offers us, at best, the accelerationism of Reagan, Thatcher, and Deng. Keynes, in contrast, offers us the glimpse of a "beyond" to capitalism—even if he wrongly thinks that capitalism itself can get us there.

Indeed, what the Bloomsbury aesthete Keynes foresees as the peaceful outcome of capitalism differs little from the utopian socialism imagined by such nineteenth-century visionaries as Charles Fourier and Oscar Wilde, among others.

Fourier and Wilde both regard the "freedom from pressing economic cares"—general affluence and elimination of the constraints of private property—as a necessary condition for human flourishing. Without the restrictions of poverty and ownership, we will be able to truly cultivate our passions (Fourier) and to pursue "Individualism" to its fullest extent (Wilde). In Wilde's description of "The Soul of Man Under Socialism,"

> while Humanity will be amusing itself, or enjoying cultivated leisure which, and not labour, is the aim of man—or making beautiful things, or reading beautiful things, or simply contemplating the world with admiration and delight, machinery will be doing all the necessary and unpleasant work.

Marx and Engels themselves, and later Marxist thinkers, tend to oppose their own "scientific socialism" to the "utopian socialism" of Fourier and others. Fourier draws up glorious plans for the future state of society that he called Harmony, but he never explains how we can possibly get there. Marx rather spends his time analyzing the contradictions of capitalism; he is notoriously skimpy on discussion of what communist society might actually be like. Nonetheless, on the rare occasions that Marx does consider the actual shape of a future communism, his vision is not all that distant from those of Fourier and Wilde—or for that matter, from Keynes's vision of affluence. In their early writings, Marx and Engels describe a society that "makes it possible for me to do one thing today and another tomorrow, to hunt in the morning, fish in the afternoon, rear cattle in the evening, criticize after dinner, just as I have a mind, without ever becoming hunter, fisherman, shepherd or critic." The Soviet cult of Stakhanovism, and other such dubious glorifications of labor in twentieth-century Marxism, have obscured the extent to which Marx's aim was not "a new distribution of labour to other persons" but rather a transformation of society that "does away with labour" altogether.

I am entirely serious, therefore, in suggesting that something like Wilde's aestheticism is a relevant model for post-capitalism. As Terry Eagleton puts it:

> The true harbinger of communism is not the proletarian but the patrician, as Oscar Wilde, a man who believed devoutly in communism in between dinner parties, was ironically aware. What better image of the indolent future than the dandy and aristocrat? Wilde thus had a wonderful political rationalization for his extravagantly privileged existence: just lie around all day in loose crimson garments reading Plato and sipping brandy and be your own communist society . . . This is why Wilde is both a convinced socialist and an unabashed aesthete, since he finds in the work of art the paradigm of the profoundly creative uselessness of communism.

Of course, we must add to this that Wilde actually still had to live in Victorian England, rather than in a communist utopia. This is why, despite his "extravagantly privileged existence," he was made to suffer in the end. In fact, Wilde's dandyism and self-fashioning is part of a longer history. Throughout the nineteenth and twentieth centuries, gay men in the West— and other minorities as well, to some extent—turned to an extravagant form of aesthetic self-cultivation, in response to the discrimination and persecution that they faced. This is not necessarily to say that such self-cultivation has ever been politically potent, or even that it can rightly be called a form of "resistance." It more often works as a secret act of secession from the dominant society than as a form of critique or protest within it. But at the very least, aesthetic self-cultivation proposes an alternative to otherwise universal standards. The tradition of gay male self-cultivation stretches, at the very least, from nineteenth-century aestheticism, through mid-twentieth-century camp, to glam rock of the 1970s, and even to Michel Foucault's late works, concerned as they are with the care and fashioning of the self.

Aesthetic self-cultivation, no less than universal affluence, is an evident absurdity in today's neoliberal world where "only the strong survive." Self-cultivation requires a climate of leisure and indolence that is incompatible, as Jonathan Crary puts it, "with the demands of a 24/7 universe." Self-cultivation is a kind of reflexive turning inward; as such, it is the opposite of self-branding, where I stylize myself in order to market myself, to be an entrepreneur of myself, and to increase the value of my "human capital." Self-cultivation is unthinkable under our current condition of austerity, where everything must be made subject to market competition and judged exclusively in terms of the financial profit that it is able to yield under stringent constraints. From an outside perspective, it is quite bizarre that we take the "discipline of the market" so much for granted, while we laugh at the supposed naiveté of Fourier's intricate calculus of passions and pleasures.

Self-cultivation also contradicts our modern (and postmodern) assumptions about the infinitude of desire. For the last century or more, we have tended to prefer an aesthetic of the sublime to one of the beautiful; or, in Roland Barthes's terms, we have tended to prefer the radical convulsions of orgasmic bliss (*jouissance*) to the easier satisfactions of mere pleasure (*plaisir*). The latter terms in both of these binaries seem complacent and quaint; they are too conservative, and too limited, to match our voracious consumerism, our aggressive boosterism, and our impulses toward rebellion and absolute negation. Today, we take it as axiomatic that—as William Blake wrote—"less than All cannot satisfy Man," and we see only disparagement in Blake's observation that "those who restrain desire do so because theirs is weak enough to be restrained."

But these are precisely the assumptions that condemn us to suffer from imposed scarcity even in the midst of plenty. Too much, as they say, is never enough. The corollary to "less than All cannot satisfy Man" is that "if any could desire what he is incapable of possessing, despair must be his eternal lot." In contrast to this vision of infinite desire, aesthetic self-cultivation always has limited aims. It makes do with the finite and the transitory. It is able to relax, with the assurance of being supported by continuing social abundance. The aesthetic of self-cultivation gladly accepts qualified and temporary satisfactions, rather than wallowing in the ironies of perpetually unfulfilled and unquenched desire.

We tend to dismiss this aestheticist vision as a naive fantasy, because we take it so much for granted that we can never really be satisfied. Rather, we continually convince ourselves that a felt sense of deprivation and scarcity will necessarily trump any measure of abundance. As Keynes says, "we have been trained too long to strive and not to enjoy." But against this, Keynes points out that the alleged insatiability of desire is itself only relative:

> Now it is true that the needs of human beings may seem to be insatiable. But they fall into two classes—those needs which are absolute in the sense that we feel them whatever the situation of

our fellow human beings may be, and those which are relative in the sense that we feel them only if their satisfaction lifts us above, makes us feel superior to, our fellows. Needs of the second class, those which satisfy the desire for superiority, may indeed be insatiable; for the higher the general level, the higher still are they. But this is not so true of the absolute needs—a point may soon be reached, much sooner perhaps than we are all of us aware of, when these needs are satisfied in the sense that we prefer to devote our further energies to non-economic purposes.

Even when it comes to competitive emulation, Keynes suggests, we will soon be able to get beyond "the love of money as a possession"—something that he regards, with Wildean disdain, as "a somewhat disgusting morbidity." The social satisfaction of "absolute needs" will allow our remaining, merely "relative" ones to be expressed in multiple, attenuated forms. Above all, we will be able to turn our efforts toward "non-economic purposes." Where neoliberalism dreams of transforming every aspect of life into a competitive marketplace, Keynes sees the good life as possible only when we are free from the pressures of such a marketplace.

I think that the neoliberal disdain for Keynes stems as much from this general attitude of his as it does from his interventionist economic policies. Far from dismissing Keynes's affluent aestheticism as just a symptom of his own narrowly upper-middle-class background, we should appreciate it as an alternative form of life for a postcapitalist world. Indeed, our own unquestioned assumptions about desire are themselves symptomatic of the contemporary state of political economy. Neoclassical economics defines itself as the study of how people make choices under conditions of scarcity. Or, to use the definition cited by Foucault: "economics is the science of human behavior as a relationship between ends and scarce means which have mutually exclusive uses." Neoclassical economics assumes infinite desires and limited resources, and examines how strategies of substitution work to maximize marginal utility under the constraint of scarcity. This was already the case for the marginalism of the later nineteenth century. The neoliberal innovation is to extend this logic beyond the traditional market economy, by using it (as Foucault says) "to decipher non-market relationships and phenomena which are not strictly and specifically economic but what we call social phenomena."

Neoclassical economics, and *a fortiori* its neoliberal extension, is thus founded upon a weird metaphysical dualism. On the one hand, desire itself is unlimited and intrinsically ungraspable. We cannot ground it, explain it, or circumscribe it in any way. On the other hand, and at the very same time, the particular decisions impelled by this desire are themselves entirely rational and quantifiable. People's behavior exhibits their "revealed preferences," and market mechanisms work to give a uniform standard of value by pricing all the alternatives. This transformation—from the negativity of unqualifiable desire to the quantitative calculability of "choices" made under the constraint of the price system—reproduces the way that capitalism as a whole both produces abundance, and ceaselessly transforms it into scarcity.

Keynes only breaks in part with the logic of neoclassical economics. But the classical economics of Smith and especially Ricardo, which provides the basis for Marx's critique of political economy, is revived in the twentieth century by Keynes's colleague and friend Piero Sraffa. The revived classical approach is quite different from the neoclassical one. Classical economics is concerned not with individual decisions made under constraints of scarcity but with social production, distribution, and expenditure. It examines how a society can materially reproduce itself, and how it can grow by generating a surplus. It is therefore directly concerned with the production, management, and distribution of such a surplus. Classical economics thus assumes abundance rather than scarcity. Its implicit metaphysics avoids the dualism of infinite desire on the one hand and "rational choice" on the other. Instead, classical economics assumes an interplay—involving both accommodation and conflict—among various finitely positive forces. It thereby opens up a space for multiple living arrangements and forms of self-cultivation—instead of submitting everything to the ruthless trials of competition.

In our current age of capitalist realism, and of what may well be called the metaphysics of desire, this ethos of surplus and self-cultivation seems bizarre, alien, and nearly unimaginable. Yet it makes sense as a response to the abundance that capitalism actually produces, though without allowing us to partake of it. This is why I see such an ethos as a necessary component of any accelerationism worthy of the name. Aesthetic reflection and self-cultivation is every bit as crucial to a postcapitalist future as is the political project of "collective self-mastery," and economic planning and modeling, urged upon us by Williams and Srnicek in their Manifesto. In particular, the very real prospect of posthumanism and transhumanism—that is to say, of technological alterations of the very nature of what it means to be "human"—must be considered in aesthetic terms rather than only utilitarian ones. Radical self-transformation is unavoidably problematic, since it involves changing the very "self" that wills the transformation in the first place. If posthuman self-alteration is not folded into an aesthetic of self-cultivation, then it will only be answerable to the programs of large corporations.

Environmental concerns as well need to be posed in terms of surplus rather than scarcity. Ecology should not be confused with austerity. We must learn not to live with less but to partake more fully of the Sun's overabundant bounty and to dissipate its gifts more widely. Our current devastation of the biosphere is itself best understood as another form of imposed scarcity, stemming from our fantasies of the violent negativity of desire.

Of course, all this still leaves unanswered the question of how we get from here to there. Is it possible to accelerate the bounty of the forces of production without also accelerating the violent destructiveness and imposed scarcity of the relations of production? I conclude with an accelerationist fable that pushes both of these tendencies to the bitter end. Paul Di Filippo's science fiction short story "Phylogenesis" confronts the full monstrosity of Capital and especially of the ecological catastrophe that is one of its chief consequences. But it is also a story about *living on* in the face of this monstrosity, and finding a bounty even in straightened circumstances. As the story promises us, from the beginning: "Life is tenacious, life is ingenious, life is mutable, life is fecund."

The literal premise of "Phylogenesis" is that an alien species of enormous "invaders came to Earth from space without warning . . . In blind fulfillment of their life cycle, they sought biomass for conversion to more of their kind." As a result, "the ecosphere had been fundamentally disrupted, damaged beyond repair." The invaders' massive predation leaves the Earth a barren, ruined mass: "the planet, once green and blue, now resembled a white featureless ball, exactly the texture and composition of the [invading species]."

Human beings are reluctant to accept the hard truth that they cannot repel the invasion: "only in the final days of the plague, when the remnants of mankind huddled in a few last redoubts, did anyone admit that extermination of the invaders and reclamation of the planet was impossible." The human agenda is reset at the last possible moment: with victory unattainable, sheer survival becomes the only remaining goal. In this situation of general destruction, there is no longer any environment capable of sustaining humanity. It is necessary, instead, "to adapt a new man to the alien conditions."

And so "the chromosartors begin to work," genetically refashioning *Homo sapiens* into a new species. We are reborn as viral parasites, living within the very bodies of the space-faring invaders. On the outside, the host presents a smooth surface: it is a "tremendous glaucous bulk," with skin "like a bluish-gray compound of fat and plastic," possessed of "a relatively high albedo," and shaped like a "featureless ovoid." But a whole ecology pullulates beneath "the sleek uniformity of the host's thick skin." Its "interior structure" is "a labyrinth of cells and arteries, nerves and organs, structural tubules and struts . . . A nonhomogeneous environment of wet and dry spaces, some cluttered with pulsing conduits and organs, some home to roving organelles, others like the empty caverns formed in foam." This is where the genetically refashioned human species takes up residence.

This monstrous host is oddly reminiscent of what Deleuze and Guattari call the *body without organs*. This is, in one of its dimensions, the *socius*, or "recording surface" that appropriates to itself the entire social product. In our current conditions, the body without organs is the monstrous body of Capital itself. Deleuze and Guattari tell us that the body without organs "presents its smooth, slippery, opaque, taut surface as a barrier." But beneath this smooth surface, it "senses there are larvae and loathsome worms . . . so many nails piercing the flesh, so many forms of torture." In a primary sense, capital is parasitic (or "vampiric") because it lives and grows by expropriating the products of living labor. But in a secondary, existential sense, predatory capital is the basic fact of our existence, and we can only survive by becoming, in turn, parasitic upon it.

Most of the text of "Phylogenesis" lovingly recounts the physiology, psychology, and overall life cycle of the new parasitic humanity. The bioengineering is precise and efficient. Everything is optimized in accordance with the physiology and metabolism of the host, and in the interest of maximal flexibility. Anything deemed superfluous to survival is unsentimentally jettisoned. The "neohumans" mate quickly, reproduce in great numbers (in "litters" of five or more), and mature rapidly. They exhibit both swarm behavior—ganging up together when necessary, in order to overwhelm the host's defenses—and nomadic distribution—"scattering themselves throughout the interior of the gargantuan alien" to reduce the chances of being all wiped out at once by the host's counterattacks.

Once the neohumans have lived off and finally killed their host, completing a generational life cycle, they go into hibernation within "protective vesicles," in order to survive the vacuum of deep space until they can encounter another host. In this way, they are able to perpetuate both their genes and their cultural heritage. Since they unavoidably "possess a basically nonmaterial culture," they only use lightweight technologies that have been interiorized within their bodies. They are especially gifted with "mathematical skill," including a genetically instilled "predisposition toward solving . . . abstruse functions in their heads." Aesthetically, they are all masters and lovers of song, "the only art form left to the artifact-free neohumans."

Mathematics and music are the sole "legacy of six thousand years of civilization" that has been bequeathed to them. The lives of the neohumans are short and intermittent; they are "mayflies, fast-fading blooms, the little creatures of a short hour. Yet to themselves, their lives still tasted sweet as of old."

Di Filippo's story turns upon devising a brilliant strategy for *adapting to* capitalism's catastrophic monstrosity. When "There Is No Alternative"—when it no longer seems possible for us to defeat the monstrous invasion, or even to imagine things otherwise, this parasitic inversion is the best that we can do. The neohumans of "Phylogenesis" evade extinction at the hands of the monstrous aliens and accelerate their own evolution in response to the accelerated reproduction of Capital. They end up devising a situation in which their own survival absolutely depends on the continuing survival of the monstrosities as well. Can they even imagine the monsters going away? "We can't count on it, we can't even dream about it." The parasitic neohumans end up killing whatever host they have invaded, but their continuing proliferation is always contingent upon encountering another host. The extinction of the invaders would mean their own definitive extinction as well.

As far as I can determine, Di Filippo did not intend "Phylogenesis" to be read as an allegory of Capital. Yet the marks are there in every aspect of the story. The downsizing of the neohumans (adults are "four feet tall, with limbs rather gracile than muscular"), the rationalization of their design in the interest of mobility and flexibility, their uncanny coordination and ability to "monitor the passage of time with unerring precision, thanks to long-ago modifications in the suprachiasmatic nuclei of their brains, which provided them with accurate biological clocks," the "inbuilt determinism" by means of which their sexual drives are canalized "for a particular purpose," their severely streamlined cultural heritage, and the ways that even their nonproductive activities (singing and nonprocreative sex) serve a purpose as "supreme weapons in the neohumans' armory of spirit": all of these are recognizable variations of familiar management techniques in our contemporary post-Fordist regime of flexible accumulation. The neohumans make use of the only tools that they find at hand; they mimic and parasitize the very mechanisms that have dispossessed them.

The emotional lives of the neohumans are effectively streamlined in a post-Fordist manner as well. Feeling an overwhelming sense of loss, and aware of all the ways that their potential has been constrained, these people see no hope of things ever getting better. But they conclude that "we just have to make the most of the life we have." Both materially and affectively, they develop an ethos of abundance, generosity, and self-cultivation, even in the face of terror and dispossession. This is, finally, what we must learn to accelerate.

Notes

Introduction to Accelerationism

Benjamin Noys: Noys 2010, Noys 2014.
Alex Williams and Nick Srnicek: Williams and Srnicek 2013.
Hyperbolic Futures: Shaviro 2011.
Pop Apocalypse: Konstantinou 2009.
Bertolt Brecht: Benjamin 1998, 121.
Science fiction as extrapolation: Shaviro 2003.
The virtual: Deleuze 1994.
Tendential processes: Marx 1993, Part III (chapters 13–15).
Real without being actual: Deleuze 1994, 208.
The Communist Manifesto: Marx and Engels 2002.
Parallax: Karatani 2003, Žižek 2006.
At a certain stage of development: Marx 1979.
Event versus situation: cf. Badiou 2013.
Audre Lord: Lorde 2007, 110–14.
Jameson on capitalism today: Jameson 2011, 9.
Neoliberalism: Foucault 2008; Harvey 2007.
Even our sleep: Crary 2013.
Hyperobjects: Morton 2013.

Networks of media technologies: Hansen 2014.

Capitalism's self-renewal through crisis: Harvey 2011, 215.

Sheer aimless infinity: Bloch 1986, 140.

Uncertainty versus risk: Keynes 1937.

Hyperchaos: Meillassoux 2008, 101–7.

Black-Scholes Formula: cf. Ayache 2010.

Efficient Market Hypothesis: see the analyais in Henwood 1998.

Affirmative speculation: uncertain commons 2013.

Premediation: Grusin 2010.

Capitalist realism: Fisher 2009.

Network society: Castells 2000; Shaviro 2003.

Small is beautiful: Schumacher 2010.

Bridge to the eighteenth century: Postman 2000.

Noys on accelerationism: Noys 2010. For a more recent and focused discussion, see Noys 2014.

Anti-Oedipus: Deleuze and Guattari 1983.

Libidinal Economy: Lyotard 1993.

To go further still: Deleuze and Guattari 1983.

Nick Land: Land 2011.

Creative destruction: Schumpeter 1984.

Virulent nihilism: Land 1991.

Deleuze on alienation and exploration: Deleuze 1990, 161.

Manifesto: Williams and Srnicek 2013.

Jameson on Wal-Mart: Jameson 2009, chapter 16 (410–34).

McLuhan on media potentials: McLuhan 1994.

Cavell on the possibilities of a medium: Cavell 1979, 31–32.

Catallaxy: Hayek 1978, 107–32.

Men make their own history: Marx 1994.

Realms of necessity and freedom: Marx 1993, chapter 48.

Stubborn fact: Whitehead 1978, 43.

Wounds of the Spirit: Hegel 1977, 407.

Alliances: Latour 1988.

Barrier of capitalist production: Deleuze and Guattari 1983, 231, citing Marx 1993, chapter 15, section 2. (In the translation of *Capital* Volume 3 that I am using here, the citation reads:"the *true barrier* to capitalist production is *capital itself*").

Market Forces: Morgan 2005.

Foucault on neoliberal competition: Foucault 2008, 120.

Woken Furies: Morgan 2007.

Kurt Russell movie: cf. Kurt Russell as Snake Plissken in John Carpenter's
 Escape from New York (1981) and *Escape from L.A.* (196).

Accelerationist Aesthetics

Tout se résume dans l'Esthétique et l'Économie politique: Mallarmé 1895.

Determination in the last instance: Althusser 2006, 123.

Aesthetics becomes first philosophy: Harman 2007, 205.

Kant on aesthetic judgment: Kant 2000. Disinterest, 91 and 96. Enjoying
 cuisine, 96. Enjoyment in safety, 144. Noncognitive, 215–16.

Escapism versus escape: Miéville 2000.

Wittgenstein on inner experience: Wittgenstein 1953. Wheel as useless
 mechanism, 101 (section 271). Not a something but not a nothing either:
 109 (section 304).

Formal and real subsumption: Marx 2004, Appendix, 943–1084; Hardt
 and Negri 2001, 24–25.

Vampire-like: Marx 2004, 342.

An entrepreneur of himself: Foucault 2008, 226.

The common: Hardt 2010.

A veritable Kantian Antinomy of the aesthetic: by analogy to Kant's Antinomy of Pure Reason, Kant 1998, 459–550.

Aesthetic production today: Jameson 1990, 4–5.

Aesthetics as unique selling point: Postrel 2004, 2, quoting an unnamed
 business executive.

Affective labor: Hardt and Negri 2001.

Impalpable commodities: Biehl-Missal and Saren 2012.

Cognitive capitalism: Moulier Boutang 2012.

Tendential fall of the rate of profit: Marx 1993, Part III (chapters 13–15).

Financial derivatives with no underlying: Ayache 2010.

Thresholds, intensities, and modulations: Deleuze 1997, 177–82 ("Post-
 script on Control Societies").

Push it to the limit: James 2012.

No external standpoint: Hardt and Negri 2001, 32.

New spirit of capitalism: Boltanski and Chiapello 2007.

The most intense lives: James 2012.

Deleuze on Nietzsche: Deleuze 2004, 258.

Neveldine and Taylor's Gamer: for an extended discussion, see Shaviro 2010, 93–130.

Enlightened cynicism: Sloterdijk 1988.

Excess as overdrive of normality: James forthcoming.

Hotshot: Peter Watts, "Hotshot," in Strahan 2014 (n.p.).

Koch brothers: Pareen 2014; Valentine 2014; Abrams 2014.

Justice instinct: Watts 2014.

"The People of Sand and Slag": Bacigalupi 2010, 49–68.

Capitalist realism: Fisher 2009.

Parasites on the Body of Capital

La politique du pire: Noys 2010, 5.

Constant revolutionizing: Marx and Engels 2002.

Disenchantment: "Science as a Vocation," in Weber 2004.

Intelligibility detached from meaning: Brassier 2011b.

Science as the construction of inferential links: Brassier 2011a.

The expropriators are expropriated: Marx 2004, 929.

No one has ever died of contradictions: Deleuze and Guattari 1983, 151. Thanks to Wolfendale 2014 for reminding me of this citation.

Bad infinity: Hegel 2010, 109 and passim.

Capital as vampire: Marx 2004, 342.

Violent destruction of capital: Marx 1973, 749–50.

The deliberate creation of lack: Deleuze and Guattari 1983, 28.

Epidemic of overproduction: Marx and Engels 2002.

The future is already here: This quotation is so widely cited, and in so many contexts, that it is impossible to give a single source. Apparently William Gibson did say it, on multiple occasions. Its first use is unknown.

Keynes on the economic problem: Keynes 1930, 364 and 366–67.

The unemployed person's hopes for his great-grandchildren: Schumpeter 1984, 145.

Hayek versus Keynes: Skidelsky 2006.

Cultivating the passions: Fourier 1972.

The Soul of Man under Socialism: Wilde 2001, 141 and passim.

One thing today and another tomorrow: Marx and Engels 1998, 53.

Doing away with labor: Marx and Engels 1998, 60.

Eagleton on Wilde: "Communism: Lear or Gonzalo?" In Douzinas and
    Žižek 2010, 104 and 101–9.

Foucault's late works: See, e.g., "The Ethics of the Concern of the Self as a
    Practice of Freedom," in Foucault 1998, 281–301.

24/7 universe: Crary 2013, 10.

Self-branding: Beals 2008.

Sublime versus beautiful: See Shaviro 2009, 1–16, and Shaviro 2014, 43.

Bliss versus pleasure: Barthes 1975.

Less than All cannot satisfy Man: "There is No Natural Religion [b]," in
    Blake 1997, 2.

Those who restrain desire: "The Marriage of Heaven and Hell," in Blake
    1997, 34.

Desire what he is incapable of possessing: "There is No Natural Religion
    [b]," in Blake 1997, 2.

Striving versus enjoying: Keynes 1930, 368.

Insatiable needs: Keynes 1930, 365.

Love of money as a disgusting morbidity: Keynes 1930, 369.

Economics as science of human behavior: cited in Foucault 2008, 222.

Extension of economics to noneconomic phenomena: Foucault 2008, 240.

Piero Sraffa: Sraffa 1960.

Capitalist realism: Fisher 2009.

"Manifesto for an Accelerationist Politics": Williams and Srnicek 2013.

Posthumanism and transhumanism: See Roden 2012.

"Phylogenesis": Di Filippo 2002, 43–57.

Body without organs: Deleuze and Guattari 1983, 7–16.

Bibliography

Abrams, Lindsay. 2014. "The Koch Brothers Are Going After Solar Panels." In *Salon*, April 21, 2014. http://www.salon.com/2014/04/21/the_koch_brothers_are_going_after_solar_panels/.

Althusser, Louis, 2006. *For Marx*. Trans. Ben Brewster. New York: Verso.

Ayache, Elie. 2010. *The Blank Swan: The End of Probability*. Hoboken, N.J.: Wiley.

Bacigalupi, Paolo. 2010. *Pump Six and Other Stories*. San Francisco: Night Shade Books.

Badiou, Alain. 2013. *Ethics: An Essay on the Understanding of Evil*. Trans. Peter Hallward. New York: Verso.

Barthes, Roland. 1975. *The Pleasure of the Text*. Trans. Richard Miller. New York: Hill & Wang.

Beals, Jeff. 2008. *Self Marketing Power: Branding Yourself as a Business of One*. Omaha: Keynote Publishing.

Benjamin, Walter. 1998. *Understanding Brecht*. Trans. Anna Bostock. New York: Verso.

Biehl-Missal, Brigitte, and Michael Saren. 2012. "Atmospheres of Seduction: A Critique of Aesthetic Marketing Practices." *Journal of Macromarketing*, February 1, 2012.

Blake, William. 1997. *The Complete Poetry & Prose of William Blake*, Revised Edition. New York: Anchor.

Bloch, Ernst. 1986. *The Principle of Hope*. Trans. Neville Plaice, Stephen Plaice, and Paul Knight. Cambridge, Mass.: MIT Press.

Boltanski, Luc, and Eve Chiapello. 2007. *The New Spirit of Capitalism.* Trans. Gregory Elliott. New York: Verso.

Brassier, Ray. 2011a. "The View from Nowhere." *Identities: Journal for Politics, Gender, and Culture* 8, no. 2.

———. 2011b. "I Am a Nihilist Because I Still Believe in Truth." Available online at. http://www.kronos.org.pl/index.php?23151,896

Castells, Manuel. 2000. *The Rise of the Network Society.* Volume 1 of *The Information Age: Economy, Society, and Culture,* 2nd ed. Malden, Mass.: Blackwell.

Cavell, Stanley. 1979. *The World Viewed: Reflections on the Ontology of Film,* Enlarged edition. Cambridge, Mass.: Harvard University Press.

Crary, Jonathan. 2013. *24/7: Late Capitalism and the Ends of Sleep.* New York: Verso.

Deleuze, Gilles. 1990. *The Logic of Sense.* Trans. Mark Lester. New York: Columbia University Press.

———. 1994. *Difference and Repetition.* Trans. Paul Patton. New York: Columbia University Press.

———. 1997. *Negotiations: 1972–1990.* Trans. Martin Joughin. New York: Columbia University Press.

———. 2004. *Desert Islands and Other Texts, 1953–1974.* Ed. David Lapoujade. Trans. Mike Taormina. Los Angeles: Semiotext(e).

Deleuze, Gilles, and Félix Guattari. 1983. *Anti-Oedipus.* Trans. Robert Hurley, Mark Seem, and Helen R. Lane. Minneapolis: University of Minnesota Press.

Di Filippo, Paul. 2002. *Babylon Sisters and Other Posthumans.* Canton, Ohio: Prime Books.

Douzinas, Costas, and Slavoj Žižek, eds. 2010. *The Idea of Communism.* New York: Verso.

Fisher, Mark. 2009. *Capitalist Realism: Is There No Alternative?* Winchester: Zero Books.

Foucault, Michel. 1998. *Ethics: Subjectivity and Truth (Essential Works of Foucault, 1954–1984, Vol. 1).* Ed. Paul Rabinow. New York: The New Press.

———. 2008. *The Birth of Biopolitics (Lectures at the College De France).* Trans. Graham Burchell. New York: Palgrave Macmillan.

Fourier, Charles. 1972. *The Utopian Vision of Charles Fourier: Selected Texts on Work, Love, and Passionate Attraction*. Trans. and ed. Jonathan Beecher and Richard Bienvenue. Boston: Houghton Mifflin.

Grusin, Richard. 2010. *Premediation: Affect and Mediality after 9/11*. New York: Palgrave Macmillan.

Hansen, Mark B. N. 2014. *Feed-Forward: On the Future of Twenty-First-Century Media*. Chicago: University of Chicago Press.

Hardt, Michael. 2010. "The Common in Communism." *Rethinking Marxism* 22, no. 3 (July 2010).

Hardt, Michael, and Antonio Negri. 2001. *Empire*. Cambridge, Mass.: Harvard University Press.

Harman, Graham. 2007. "On Vicarious Causation." In *Collapse: Philosophical Research and Development* 2:171–205.

Harvey, David. 2007. *A Brief History of Neoliberalism*. New York: Oxford University Press.

———. 2011. *"The Enigma of Capital" and "The Crises of Capitalism."* New York: Oxford University Press.

Hayek, Friedrich A. 1978. *Law, Legislation, and Liberty, Volume 2: The Mirage of Social Justice*. Chicago: University of Chicago Press.

Hegel, G. W. F. 1977. *Phenomenology of Spirit*. Trans. A. V. Miller. New York: Oxford University Press.

———. 2010. *The Science of Logic*. Trans. George Di Giovanni. New York: Cambridge University Press.

Henwood, Doug. 1998. *Wall Street*. New York: Verso.

James, Robin. 2012. "Loving the Alien." *The New Inquiry*, October 22, 2012. http://thenewinquiry.com/essays/loving-the-alien/.

James, Robin. Forthcoming. *Resilience and Melancholy: Pop Music, Feminism, Neoliberalism*. Winchester, U.K.: Zero Books.

Jameson, Fredric. 1990. *Postmodernism, or, The Cultural Logic of Late Capitalism*. Durham, N.C.: Duke University Press.

———. 2009. *Valences of the Dialectic*. New York: Verso.

———. 2011. *Representing "Capital": A Reading of Volume One*. New York: Verso.

Kant, Immanuel. 1998. *Critique of Pure Reason*. Trans. Paul Guyer and Allen W. Wood. New York: Cambridge University Press.

———. 2000. *Critique of the Power of Judgment.* Trans. Paul Guyer and Eric Matthews. New York: Cambridge University Press.

Karatani, Kojin. 2003. *Transcritique: On Kant and Marx.* Trans. Sabu Kohso. Cambridge, Mass.: MIT Press.

Keynes, John Maynard. 1930. "Economic Possibilities for Our Grandchildren." In *Essays in Persuasion,* 358–73 New York: Norton, 1963.

———. 1937. "The General Theory of Employment." *The Quarterly Journal of Economics* 51, no. 2 (February 1937): 209–23.

Konstantinou, Lee. 2009. *Pop Apocalypse.* New York: Harper Perennial.

Land, Nick. 1991. *The Thirst for Annihilation: Georges Bataille and Virulent Nihilism.* New York: Routledge.

———. 2011. *Fanged Noumena: Collected Writings 1987–2007.* Falmouth, U.K.: Urbanomic.

Latour, Bruno. 1988. *The Pasteurization of France.* Trans. Alan Sheridan and John Law. Cambridge, Mass.: Harvard University Press.

Lorde, Audre. 2007. *Sister Outsider: Essays and Speeches.* New York: The Crossing Press.

Lyotard, Jean-François. 1993. *Libidinal Economy.* Trans. Iain Hamilton Grant. Bloomington: Indiana University Press.

Mackay, Robin, and Armen Avanessian, eds. 2014. *#Accelerate: The Accelerationist Reader.* Falmouth, U.K.: Urbanomic.

Mallarmé, Stephane. 1895. *La musique et les lettres.* http://fr.wikisource.org/wiki/La_Musique_et_les_Lettres.

Marx, Karl. 1973. *Grundrisse.* Trans. Martin Nicolaus. New York: Penguin.

———. 1979. *A Contribution to the Critique of Political Economy.* New York: International Publishers.

———. 1993. *Capital: A Critique of Political Economy, Volume 3.* Trans. David Fernbach. New York: Penguin.

———. 1994. *The Eighteenth Brumaire of Louis Bonaparte.* New York: International Publishers.

———. 2004. *Capital: A Critique of Political Economy, Volume 1.* Trans. Ben Fowkes. New York: Penguin.

Marx, Karl, and Friedrich Engels. 1998. *The German Ideology.* Amherst, N.Y.: Prometheus Books.

———. 2002. *The Communist Manifesto.* New York: Penguin.

McLuhan Marshall. 1994. *Understanding Media: The Extensions of Man.* Cambridge, Mass.: MIT Press. Originally published 1964.

Meillassoux, Quentin. 2008. *After Finitude: An Essay on the Necessity of Contingency.* Trans. Ray Brassier. New York: Continuum.

Miéville, China. 2000. "Fantasy and Revolution: An Interview with China Miéville." http://pubs.socialistreviewindex.org.uk/isj88/new singer.htm.

Morgan, Richard K. 2005. *Market Forces.* New York: Ballantine Books.
———. 2007. *Woken Furies.* New York: Del Rey.

Morton, Timothy. 2013. *Hyperobjects: Philosophy and Ecology after the End of the World.* Minneapolis: University of Minnesota Press.

Moulier Boutang, Yann. 2012. *Cognitive Capitalism.* Cambridge: Polity.

Noys, Benjamin. 2010. *The Persistence of the Negative: A Critique of Contemporary Continental Theory.* Edinburgh: Edinburgh University Press.
———. 2014. *Malign Velocities: Accelerationism and Capitalism.* Winchester, U.K.: Zero Books.

Pareen, Alex. 2014. "Koch Brothers vs. a Bus: Why Two Billionaires Hate a Transit project in Nashville." *Salon,* April 1, 2014. http://www.salon.com/2014/04/01/why_are_the_kochs_trying_to_stop_a_transit_project_in_nashville/.

Postman, Neil. 2000. *Building a Bridge to the 18th Century: How the Past Can Improve Our Future.* New York: Vintage.

Postrel, Virginia. 2004. *The Substance of Style: How the Rise of Aesthetic Value Is Remaking Commerce, Culture, and Consciousness.* New York: Harper Perennial.

Roden, David. 2012. "Humanism, Transhumanism, and Posthumanism." https://www.academia.edu/353704/Humanism_Transhumanism_and_Posthumanism.

Schumacher, E. F. 2010. *Small Is Beautiful: Economics as if People Mattered.* New York: Harper Perennial.

Schumpeter, Joseph. 1984. *Capitalism, Socialism, and Democracy.* New York: Harper.

Shaviro, Steven. 2003. *Connected, or, What It Means to Live in the Network Society.* Minneapolis: University of Minnesota Press.

———. 2009. *Without Criteria: Kant, Whitehead, Deleuze, and Aesthetics.* Cambridge, Mass.: MIT Press.

———. 2010. *Post-Cinematic Affect.* Winchester, U.K.: Zero Books.

———. 2011. "Hyperbolic Futures: Speculative Finance and Speculative Fiction." In *Cascadia Subduction Zone* 1, no. 2 (April 2011).

———. 2014. *The Universe of Things: On Speculative Realism.* Minneapolis: University of Minnesota Press.

Skidelsky, Robert. 2006. "Hayek versus Keynes: The Road to Reconciliation." http://www.skidelskyr.com/site/article/hayek-versus-keynes-the-road-to-reconciliation/.

Sloterdijk, Peter. 1988. *Critique of Cynical Reason.* Minneapolis: University of Minnesota Press.

Sraffa, Piero. 1960. *Production of Commodities by Means of Commodities: Prelude to a Critique of Economic Theory.* New York: Cambridge University Press.

Strahan, Jonathan, ed. 2014. *Reach for Infinity.* Oxford: Solaris Books.

uncertain commons. 2013. *Speculate This!* Durham, N.C.: Duke University Press.

Valentine, Katie. 2014. "Koch Brothers Quietly Seek to Ban New Mass Transit in Tennessee." http://thinkprogress.org/climate/2014/04/01/3421088/koch-brothers-tennessee/.

Watts, Peter. 2014. "The Scorched Earth Society." http://www.rifters.com/real/shorts/TheScorchedEarthSociety-transcript.pdf.

Weber, Max. 2004. *The Vocation Lectures.* Trans. Rodney Livingstone. Indianapolis: Hackett.

Whitehead, Alfred North. 1978. *Process and Reality.* New York: The Free Press.

Wilde, Oscar. 2001. *The Soul of Man under Socialism and Selected Critical Prose.* Ed. Linda Dowling. New York: Penguin Classics.

Williams, Alex, and Nick Srnicek. 2013. *#ACCELERATE MANIFESTO for an Accelerationist Politics.* http://criticallegalthinking.com/2013/05/14/accelerate-manifesto-for-an-accelerationist-politics/. Reprinted in Mackay and Avenessian 2014, 376–62.

Wittgenstein, Ludwig. 1953. *Philosophical Investigations.* 4th edition.

Trans. G. E. M. Anscombe, P. M. S. Hacker, and Joachim Schulte. Malden, Mass.: Wiley-Blackwell.

Wolfendale, Pete. 2014. "So, Accelerationism, What's All That About?" http://deontologistics.tumblr.com/post/91953882443/so-accelerationism-whats-all-that-about.

Žižek, Slavoj. 2006. *The Parallax View*. Cambridge, Mass.: MIT Press.

Steven Shaviro is DeRoy Professor of English at Wayne State University and author of *The Universe of Things: On Speculative Realism* (Minnesota, 2014), *Without Criteria: Kant, Whitehead, Deleuze, and Aesthetics* (2009), *Connected, or What It Means to Live in the Network Society* (Minnesota, 2003), and *The Cinematic Body* (Minnesota, 1993).